Dangerous Subversive Heresies

Examinations of Politics, Religion and Sex Guaranteed
to Irritate and Aggravate Both the Right and the Left

Tim Retallack

To all the family and friends who have read bits and pieces of this book over the years, and gave me nothing but encouragement to finish it.

Table of Contents

Introduction

After a lot of thought, I have developed a theory about the cause of much of the conflict among people in our society today. I think a lot of it has to do with mojo.

You can see it in the way people drive their cars. It's almost become an unwritten rule of the road; when you activate your turn signal, wait the appropriate distance, and then switch lanes ahead of another driver, they *must* pass you, in order to demonstrate how much you've inconvenienced them, even if they have to go ninety miles an hour to do it. Why? Because by pulling in front of them, *you took a little bit of their mojo*, and they have to get it back. Evidently, like self-esteem, you're only born with just so much mojo, and once it's gone, it's gone.

You can also see it in the way people confront each other face to face. If one person says something that rubs someone the wrong way, that second person feels injured. The first person has taken some of the other's mojo. Now, not only do they have to get it back, they have to take a little bit of the first person's mojo as well, as just compensation for their injury. This of course leaves the first person injured, and they must take the same action. You can see that this sets up a downward spiral, with each person taking bigger and bigger chunks of mojo, until in rare cases, it can end up with someone getting stabbed or shot.

Other people decide to just get it over with in one fell swoop. They think the way to make their point is just to take *all* of their opponent's mojo on a massive blitzkrieg-like attack, so that they have none left to fight with. And that of course, means the correct side has won the argument, doesn't it?

Examples like these led me to develop another theory about discussing important issues in our society today: *Whoever screams the loudest is right.* At least, that seems to be the trend we're following, and in the last several years in particular, the trend seems to be increasing at an exponential rate.

Well, I did not write this book to steal anyone's mojo. This book is about confronting ideas, not attacking people. The truth is, no one can steal your mojo unless you decide to let them. They haven't stolen your mojo when *they* think they've stolen it, they've only stolen your mojo when **you** think they've stolen it. Your mojo is strong and plentiful.

Stolen mojo aside, I'm under no illusions that this book is not going to rub anyone the wrong way; I think it most definitely will, but again, that is not its *intent.* It is really the documented result of years of thinking. One day several years ago (and I could not pin down the date to save my life) I just started thinking, and I kept on thinking and I just kind of couldn't stop. It was really a question that got the whole thing started: How do I *know* that what I know is right? If a piece of information jives with your philosophy, does that make it right? If you trust the person who gave it to you, does *that* make it right? If at first glance, it doesn't violate any of your principles, does *that* make it right? If it toes the line of whichever party you're registered with, does *that* make it right? Or, does it just need to make sense given everything else you know right now to be right?

After a while, my thinking started to take the form of debates inside my own head. Not having anyone else to debate with, I started taking both sides of the argument, and it was only after the most heated debates with my own devil's advocate that I felt I really understood the subject, and I really knew where I stood on it. I concluded that the way to confirm the validity or accuracy of an idea is not to perform a five second fact-check completely within the confines of your own brain, but to do exactly the opposite. If you really want to know if an idea will stand up, you have to do everything you can to tear it down. You must attack it from every conceivable angle and don't stop until you've run out of angles. If it survives your best attempts to destroy it, there is a much, much higher probability that it is the truth. Then, do some research on it, because what we know is a tiny drop in the bucket of what we don't know, and chances are considerable that what we think we know is wrong.

I'll give you an example. One of my favorite trivia questions used to be: Did Abraham Lincoln like broccoli? No matter what anyone answered, I would say "Ha, it's a trick question because broccoli didn't exist in Abraham Lincoln's time. That's because broccoli is actually a hybrid of coli flour and asparagus. It was invented by Albert R. Broccoli, who after a career change went on to produce all the early James Bond films." I believed that until I did just a little bit of research. I found out that broccoli is not a hybrid and has been around for thousands of years. What I assumed to be the truth for years was just plain wrong.

I've put many hours of research into the subjects I've written about, yet you'll notice there is not a single footnote in this book. That's because *it's a book and not a term paper!* Instead, I give you this solemn pledge, which I will here and now swear on the lives of my family: *I have not put a single idea or piece of information into this book that I **know** to be untrue.* If anyone can demonstrate that I'm mistaken about anything I've written about with empirical evidence and sound logic, I will acknowledge the fact and change my thinking. I've done it before, and I can give you an example of that too.

For anyone who is not familiar with a supreme court decision called Citizens United vs. FEC from 2010, here's the nutshell version. (This particular explanation comes from the SCOTUSblog website, if you'd like to look it up for yourself): The Supreme Court ruled that the government cannot keep corporations (and presumably labor unions) from spending money to support or denounce individual candidates in elections. While the business entities may not give money directly to the campaigns, they may seek to persuade the public through other means including ads, especially where these ads are not broadcast. Why? Because the First Amendment guarantees freedom of speech, and political spending is considered a form of free speech.

This is where the whole "Corporations are people too!" hullabaloo came from. To anyone who insisted that corporations are *not* people, I would say: "Name a single corporation that consists entirely of robots?" Of course corporations are made up of people. Now, if you put someone who has something to say in a room with one hundred other people, and then tell them that they are not allowed to speak to half of them, and I'll repeat that; *not allowed to speak to half of them*, does that person have freedom of speech? So, if you prohibit people from spending their own money to get their message out to as many people as they can, do they really have freedom of speech? It sounded very logical and reasonable.

I no longer hold that opinion. After a slightly emotional discussion with a close family member and thinking about it for several hours, I came to see that there are two times when politicians are bought and sold. One is through lobbying, and the other is at election time. Big corporations are not in the habit of making multi-million dollar investments on which they don't expect to make any return, and if they donate millions of dollars to a politician's campaign, or spend millions of dollars on media advertisements to get that politician elected, they're going to want just as much return on that investment as on any other. In a lot of countries, bribing a politician to do your bidding is called corruption. In this country, it's called lobbying and campaign donations. I see now that if you want to get government out of your business, you first have to *get business out of government*. Politicians are elected to represent people, not corporations. As for corporations being made up of people, that is still true, but if every single person in a corporation (or a labor union) came to the unanimous decision to support a particular candidate, there is no reason why they could not all do that *as individuals*. If it was truly a unanimous decision, the candidate would get just as much money, and there would not be the slightest hint of untowardness.

10

If it was *not* a unanimous decision, then at least some people are having their money used in ways to which they do not consent.

Wow, my first digression, and I'm not even through the introduction! My point is that I'm not above having my mind changed by a persuasive argument. This book is not a 75,000 word exposition on how I'm right, and anyone who disagrees with me is wrong.

There were also several things I left out of this book even though they would have made my points more persuasively than I could without them. I left them out for the sake of honesty. If you'd like to see one of them, go to YouTube and type in "Reagan Obama Socialism Cartoon." I would have loved to have included this story, which is presented as if it is a fictionalized retelling of an actual event, but no matter how much I tried to vet it, I couldn't find a shred of evidence that it ever actually happened.

You'll also notice that there are a lot more questions in this book than answers. Does that mean I don't have any of the answers? Not necessarily. A lot of times I do, but if you're on the fence about any particular issue, which answers are you most likely to believe; the answers you're given, or the answers you find for yourself? Personally, I believe it's the latter.

So there you have it; a few paragraphs to hopefully get you in the proper frame of mind to take in the essays on the following pages. So without further ado, let's jump in the deep end and talk about....

Racism

Several months ago I was walking down my quiet little suburban street when I came upon a ratty, rusted out SUV parked in front of a neighbor's house, covered almost from top to bottom in bumper stickers. I'm a big fan of bumper stickers. I've been known to momentarily follow dangerously close behind other cars on the highway in order to read them. They not only give you a point of view, but I think they also give you a tiny little snapshot of the owner's character. As I walked around this particular vehicle, I came to the conclusion the owner was someone I'd just as soon not know. They were obviously liberal, but I would never hold that against them. They were also evidently very young, again something that I would never fault them for. Several of the stickers however, depicted images of violence and nihilism, for which there is no room in my life. Then I came across a sticker that simple read "Racism is a fear of other cultures." That sticker accomplished its purpose admirably. It stuck in my mind and got me thinking as I continued down the street.

I don't have many hot buttons these days, but racism is one of them. I'm rather proud of the handle I've gained on my emotions over the last ten years or so. The Klu Klux Klan, Neo-Nazis, and skinheads are among the last few groups that can provoke genuine rage in me. I once told my son that although there are no slithery, tentacled abominations hiding in anyone's closet, or hairy, toothy beasts lurking outside bedroom windows, monsters are very real. They walk among us every day. They are people, yet they are just as inhuman and frightening as any nightmare.

There was something troubling about the idea that racism is about fear and not about hate. I know there are people who honestly believe that no one is evil; that there are only poor souls who are afraid or misunderstood or oppressed and everything would be all better again if we would just try to understand them and treat them nicely. There are about 170 million people who I think would disagree with that if they weren't all dead. There is evil in the world. I don't believe evil is a force apart from humanity that preys upon it, nor do I think it's our natural state, and something we have to be redeemed from. I believe evil is a state people can fall into when they don't maintain the discipline to be good, just as people become obese when they don't bother to eat right and exercise. Working as a nurse, I've seen people in such poor health that they could barely stand on their own two feet, and while some of them were victims of tragic diseases, the majority of them didn't have to end up that way. They simply didn't put forth the effort to stay healthy, but that doesn't mean ill health is their natural state.

When I first wrote this chapter, my son was seven years old. (He's now 18. How the hell did that happen?), yet he said something to me one night all those years ago that I found uncommonly insightful for someone so young. He said "You know Dad, when white people don't like black people, it's not really the color of their skin, it's the way they talk and the way they act." Before you let your blood boil, keep in mind that this was a seven-year-old boy. Cut him some slack. The more I thought about it, the more impressed I was. Here was a seven-year-old kid who evidently got it more than probably 80% of adults. He didn't have the vocabulary to express it, but my son was talking about culture. There it was again; Culture. Maybe there was something to that bumper sticker.

The simplest and best definition I've ever come across for the world "Culture" is: "Everything we pass along to our children." We pass on our knowledge of the world, our attitudes toward everything in it, the traditions of our ancestors, our ways of thinking about how to treat other people, the technologies we use, how we work, how we play, what we think about politics, religion, sex, sports, art, food, even the way we move and talk. Where do southern kids get their southern accents? From their southern parents. Where do young Catholics get their beliefs about the family roles of men and women? From their Catholic parents. It took me a good chunk of my life to really understand that. I heard the word "culture", and I thought of people going to opera houses or looking at art gallery walls with those ridiculous glasses on the end of a stick held in front of their faces.

So again, could it be true that racism is not about hate after all, but actually about fear? No, not completely. Very few things are that simple. There are some people who are just plain rotten. But could fear be *part* of the equation? Yes, I think it could be, and it would explain a lot....*a lot!*

There is a very good argument for racism *not* being about *race,* and that is, the concept of *race* has very little basis in biology, more specifically in genetics. While it's true that our "race" is contained in our genes, most people are under the impression that there is a little section on one of our chromosomes containing a little bunch of genes, all lined up next to each other in a neat little row, that determines our race. They also think that on the analogous chromosome in a different person of a different race, is a corresponding set of genes, again all lined up in a neat little row that determines *their race.* Those little sections of race genes don't exist.

Think of all the physical characteristics that supposedly make up race: skin color, hair color, hair texture, the shape of our noses, the shape of our eyes, our height, etc. Now imagine that we could take a walk among our chromosomes, hanging like strings of chili peppers in a Mexican market. The fact is, *some* of the genes that determine our skin color come from that chromosome over there, and some from this one here. A few of the genes that determine the shape of our nose come from this chromosome, a few from this one, and several from that one way over there. Our reproductive cells; the sperm and ova only contain *half* of those chromosomes. Every time we have a child, half of our individual chromosomes are lost to future generations, to be replaced by the genes of (hopefully) our spouse. The half that is lost probably contains a good many of those genes that determine the characteristics we think of as race. If half of our "race genes" are lost each generation, then the concept of race being genetic is starting to look a little shaky, isn't it? The truth is, your average white guy might very well have more in common *genetically* with

Morgan Freeman than he does with Ron Howard. You've heard it before, and I'm going to say it again. We're all just people.

If you look carefully at all the different ethnic and cultural groups in the world (and most people would be astonished at how many there really are), you'll find people with dark skin and straight hair, light skin and broad noses, and just about every conceivable combination of all the physical characteristics you *thought* determined race. No one group has a monopoly on any of them. So how do people of different races end up looking like each other? It's simple. People tend to marry and/or reproduce within their own *cultural* group, and when they do, the particular mix of genes that produces the traditional physical appearance of that group, go along for the ride. A physical "race" is preserved by culture.

So if fear of other cultures is at least a component of racism, it brings up an interesting proposition: There is a lot more *justification* for one person's fear of another's culture than hatred of the color of their skin.

Different cultures attach different values to everything. The concept of monogamy has more value in Judeo-Christian culture than in Muslim culture. Being thin is much more important in European culture than in Polynesian culture. In our American culture, we look after our children first, and yet there are some cultures in Africa where the men eat first, then the women, and if there is any left, the children eat last. If there isn't any food left for the children, well that's just the way it goes. In American culture, we're a lot more fixated on personal hygiene, particularly on *smelling nice*, than Europeans are, and there is at least one culture in Southwestern Asia in which people do not bathe at all….as in *ever*, yet that same culture considers a pregnant women to be so unclean, she is forced to live in a mud hut on the outskirts of the village until she gives birth. Then, suddenly, she is "clean" again.

In some cultures, the lives of certain people have so little value that killing them is considered acceptable. Two examples are China and India, where the practice of female infanticide is still practiced. In India, male children work in the fields and bring income into the family, and are therefore considered a sort of insurance against hard times. Female children are considered a liability, partly because according to tradition, when they get married, their family will have to pay a dowry to the family of the groom that can sometimes amount to ten times the annual salary of an Indian civil servant. Daughters are considered so worthless, you have to pay someone to take them off your hands. In isolated places in rural India, baby girls are considered nothing but a liability, and they are often either left to starve to death, poisoned, strangled, smothered or drowned.

In China, the same preference for baby boys exists, because it's believed that they will support their parents in their old age. Girls on the other hand, traditionally move in with their in-laws when they get married, and are therefore considered a liability. Their parents go the effort and expense of raising them, and get nothing from them in return. Due to China's official policy of one child per family, (This was recently rescinded, but not for the good of the family, but rather for the good of the Communist Party), when a baby girl is born, she is sometimes murdered and her parents try again for a boy. My point is this: If you were a young girl suddenly dropped into the culture of either of these countries, you would have a very *legitimate reason* to fear that culture, but does that make you a racist, and if it does, is your "racism" evil, or does it just make you human?

Now before you admonish me that these are exotic cultures on the other side of the world and have nothing to do with life here in the United States, I'd like to remind you of a three-year-old girl named Stephanie Kuhan. If you don't remember her name, you might remember what happened to her and her family in 1995, in the Cypress Park neighborhood of Los Angeles. She was riding in a car with her mother, her brother and a friend when they had the bad fortune to get lost in the territory of a Latino gang called The Avenues. They mistakenly turned into a blind alley, where members of the Avenues surrounded the car and filled it with bullets, killing Stephanie and wounding her one year old brother.

Stephanie was killed because in the gang culture of that neighborhood, her life had no value. I think she and her family had a very real and very legitimate reason to fear *that* culture, just as a young girl, dropped into the middle of rural India or China would have good reason to fear the culture there. If racism really is a fear of other cultures, then it is a lot more understandable than hatred of someone's race, and it would be unreasonable to hold that kind of fear against anyone.

Now, here's the *big* problem with *tha*t idea.

It was not *Latino* culture that killed Stephanie Kuhan, it was the culture of the Avenues gang. Fifty yards away, in the same Latino neighborhood, I can guarantee you there were people who would have done anything they could to save her. There is no one "Latino Culture." There is no one "Black Culture." There is no one "White Culture." The same culture that gives us NASCAR collector chicken buckets is not the same one that gives us the Academy Awards. The culture that gives us Gangsta Rap is not the same culture that gives us Quincy Jones.

Here is my theory on racism. Take it for what you will. The chances that we will ever be dropped into the middle of a mainstream ethnic culture in which we have absolutely no value are very, very slim. It is actually the worst elements in *any* culture that are feared by people of other cultures. When people think about racism, they mistakenly draw vertical lines between races, and then fear what's on the other sides of those lines simply because we can *see* that it's so very different. If we must draw lines, they should be horizontal lines across every race and culture, with each one's best elements; its art, it's music, it's literature, its architecture, its food, and its universal, cross-cultural instinct to help other people at the top, and each one's stereotyping, ignorance, bigotry, hatred of skin color, and callous devaluation of human life at the bottom. I promise you, the people in the very top layers of *that* spectrum will go out of their way to make you feel welcome and comfortable in their culture, exactly *because* it is so unfamiliar to you, no matter who you are.

So what's the answer? Beats me. There are some problems in this world that have no easy answer. You cannot force other cultures to value you. You can force certain individuals in other cultures to *behave as if* they do, but have you really accomplished anything by doing that? Should we strive for one homogeneous world culture in which we cannot fear the differences between us because there are none? Impossible, unless you want to live under a dictator at the point of a gun. Even if that were possible, I pray that it never happens because there is so much beauty in the best of each culture.

Some people will tell you that the United States is a racist country; that racism is deeply ingrained in our "American Culture." *If* that were true, then every one of us would witness racist acts all around us every day. We don't. Perhaps a more accurate definition of racism would be: "The mistaken and delusional belief that the worst elements of human nature occur only in *other* cultures, and not in one's own." But then again, that wouldn't fit very well on a bumper sticker, would it?

I

I am an *individual*

I am *not* "the white race."

I am *not* "the male sex."

I am not a political party or a religion.

I am one, single, solitary *individual.*

I am no one but me.

I gladly take responsibility for everything *I* do, everything *I* say, everything that results solely from *my* actions, and everything over which *I* am given sole control.

But that is where my *responsibility* ends.

So if you want me to help you right some great wrong you see in the world, I will do so of my own free will, but if you want me to *atone* for it, then I'm afraid it is up to *you* to demonstrate that I personally took part in it. If you can't do that, then I can't help you.

I am an *individual*

I am feared and loathed by Left and Right alike,
because I am so dangerous to both.

Politicians and the Media

As I write this, I'm speeding East on Interstate 70 out of the little town of Oakley Kansas. I know what you're thinking, but don't worry, I'm not driving. My wife is doing that. We're heading home to Louisville Kentucky from our yearly pilgrimage to Grand Junction Colorado, taking our time on this trip instead of driving straight through; a twenty four hour ordeal that we are increasingly loathe to undertake. The reason I mention all this is to create an opportunity to mention just one of the things that is still right with America, and that is the 1st Travel Inn, in Oakley Kansas. It is by no means a luxury hotel, but the rooms are clean and comfortable, the rates more than reasonable and the family that runs it are the nicest people you could ever want to meet. Whether or not they will consider being mentioned in a book such as this as a compliment, I can't really say, but I highly recommend staying there if you're ever passing though the area.

It was while we were in Grand Junction that I heard something that told me it was time to write this chapter. I was listening to Talk Radio 1100, the only talk radio station in Grand Junction at the time. I'm pretty sure there is no programming of local origin, but the commercials are locally produced, and it was one of these that caught my attention. I can't even tell you the guy's name or what he was selling because I was so taken aback by what he said, which was this: "Our world is getting so dangerous that we can hardly afford to sleep, and it's only going to get worse for our children." That statement irked me on a couple of levels, and I'm going to take them one at a time.

As absurd as that statement is, there are people who will believe it....way too many of them. They will take it at face value and never think for a single second to question it. That, my friends, is one of the things that is truly wrong with America. There are too many sheeple among us. There is a desperate shortage of critical thinking skills in this country, and in the world at large for that matter. I don't think it's any accident that you never, ever see a freshman college course entitled Critical Thinking 101.

Perhaps we are simply so bombarded with messages from every conceivable source that our filters have become overloaded and failed. Perhaps our lives have become so cushy and comfortable that we're no longer willing to put forth the mental effort to think things through. Perhaps we've been so indoctrinated with blind obedience to authority that we don't dare entertain the thought of questioning it. Whatever the reason, there is no shortage of people willing to exploit our gullibility. The most dangerous of these, in my opinion, are our politicians.

Neither our gullibility nor other people's propensities to capitalize on it are anything new. Propagandists have always known that if you say something often enough, people will start to believe it. Some have gone so far as to say if you repeat something often enough, it *becomes* the truth. I've noticed a disturbing development in this concept in the last several years. The number of repetitions required to achieve pseudo-truth status has been reduced to *one*. Simply state what you want people to think, and the universe magically changes to conform to your agenda.

A couple of shining examples of this have come out of our Congress. I know this is going back awhile, but in the summer of 2008, as gasoline prices rose though $4.00 a gallon for the first time, and America was sitting on top of more energy reserves than Saudi Arabia, oil company executives were summoned to Washington to answer for "what they had done to this country." (What they've actually done is make our civilization possible, but that's another discussion.) This was where then Speaker of the House Nancy Pelosi first uttered the phrase "We can't drill our way out of this one." This is the logical equivalent of telling a starving person that they can't eat their way out of being hungry, and yet *no one* confronted her. Within days, dozens of politicians, including then presidential candidate Barack Obama were repeating the new mantra. I wasn't sure what astounded me more;

that Ms. Pelosi could make such an unsupportable statement with impunity or that not a single one of the oil executives had the backbone to stand up to her.

The more I think about them, the more statements like Ms. Pelosi's beg the question: Are our politicians really that stupid, or do they think *we're* that stupid? I am dead serious when I ask this, because when statements such as this are uttered by public figures for mass consumption and are not immediately and decisively challenged, those are the only two possibilities I can come up with. Of course, politicians *do* think we're stupid They count on it. They depend on an uninformed and apathetic populace to be clay in their hands, and most politicians' grandstanding could not stand up to five minutes' application of reason and logic.

I'll give you a very recent example. One of the issues on which 2016 presidential candidate Bernie Sanders ran his campaign, was correcting the income disparity between men and women. The current figure I've heard is that women only make seventy-eight cents for every dollar men make. This figure could *only* have been arrived at by taking the total amount of money paid yearly to men, and comparing it to the total amount of money paid yearly to women. That's it. Delve any deeper into the issue, and the issue falls apart. Does anyone honestly think that if you audited the books of any 100 companies in this country, chosen at random, that you would find each and every woman in the company being paid exactly 78% of what each and every man is paid for doing the same job? On second thought, scratch that question. Obviously there *are* people who believe that. Now, I invite them to *investigate* that claim with me.

Let me ask you this: Which job pays more; clerking in a supermarket, or working on a crab boat like the ones on the reality series Deadliest Catch? I mean, those guys work for a couple of months and make $50,000.00 The clerk works all year long and makes half of that. Talk about income inequality! Why should that be? Why should the crab fishermen make so much more money than the store clerk? The answer is in the name of the TV show; *Deadliest* Catch. Working on a crab boat is one of the most dangerous jobs in the world; *that's* why it pays so much.

Now let me ask you this. If the owner of every one of those crab boats could save 22% on their labor costs every year, and make 22% more profit, don't you think they would do that? Well there's a very simple way to do it. All they would have to do is hire every woman who applies for the job and none of the men. Sounds like a no-brainer, right? I mean, they only have to pay them 78 cents for every dollar they paid the men, right? There's just one problem....*extremely few women apply to be crab fishermen....***because it's one of the most dangerous jobs in the world!** The fact is, men hold more than 90% of all the *most dangerous*, and therefore the *highest paying* jobs in this country. It's not because male employers are shutting women out, it's because most women *choose not to* go after those jobs.

Still, the concept doesn't have to apply only to crab fishing. So you have to ask; if every employer in America could save 22% on their labor costs just by hiring a woman, why would any of them ever hire a man?

Another question: Who are the highest paid employees in America? Answer: Professional Athletes. Their contracts are routinely valued in the *hundreds of millions* of dollars; *hundreds of thousands of dollars **per game***. Now wouldn't you like to save 22% of *that?* All you have to do is replace all the male athletes with females, right? So why are professional sports franchise owners not hiring exclusively women? Of course, some of them do just that, and pay them much lower salaries, which plays right into the argument about the gender income gap. Of course, women's sports teams *could* immediately start paying their athletes salaries equivalent to the NBA or the NFL....for about half a season, and then they would all go bankrupt, *because sports fans won't pay the high ticket prices needed to support NFL or NBA salaries to watch women play sports?* Now is *that* an evil conspiracy on the part of the franchise owners, or is it the combined economic choices of millions of individual sports fans?

If you correct for all relevant factors, including the kinds of jobs men go after and women don't, stay-at-home moms and women who take leaves of absence to care for infants, and how wildly exorbitant, male dominated sports salaries skew the figures, **the gender income gap does not exist**, and yet, Bernie Sanders still ran on it. Now we have to ask the question: Does Bernie Sanders *not know* everything I've just told you here? *I* know it, and I'm just a regular schmuck. Now *you* know it, but I won't make any judgments about *your* schmuckiness. So if you and I know, and Bernie Sanders is totally oblivious, *is he really smart enough to be our president?* Well, *he* obviously thinks he is.

If he *does* know these facts, and he's ran on the issue *anyway*....isn't that called *a lie?*

So why do so many of us believe the things politicians say? I believe it's because too many of us are operating under the false impression that politicians are somehow exalted. We think our elected leaders got to be our leaders because they exhibit the quality of leadership, and they are more qualified than the rest of us to do the things they do. We believe they, as a group are more experienced, more enlightened, more insightful, smarter, and operate on a higher plane than their constituents. I'd like to see some objective empirical evidence that this is so. There is really only *one* difference between you and your elected officials that can be proven in every case. *They had the money and went to the effort to get themselves elected,* **and you didn't**. They, as a group are no more intelligent than you or me, and if the things they say are any measure, many of them are considerably *less* so. Representative Sheila Jackson Lee (D-TX) once asked some NASA officials if the Mars Rovers had ever ventured over to take a picture of the American flag the astronauts left there. She also recently identified homicide as a major cause of murders in the U.S. Representative Joe Barton (R-TX) told the House Energy and Commerce Subcommittee that "The wind is a finite resource, and harnessing it will slow the wind down, which will make the temperature go up." And last but not least, Representative Hank Johnson (D-GA) expressed concern to Navy officials that if too many U.S. naval personnel were to be stationed on the island of Guam, the island might tip over and capsize. These are but a few of the intellectual powerhouses you have deciding how you should live your life.

In fact, I would make the case that in terms of morality, politicians are by and large inferior to you and me. The majority of Americans are not unapologetic liars. It can be demonstrated that the majority of politicians are. If one politician tells the truth about the way things are; if they say only what can be backed up with objective facts and empirical evidence, and another tells the voting public what they want to hear, regardless of whether or not it bears any resemblance to reality, which one is going to get re-elected? If you had a $170,000.00 job with an 80% retirement after four or six years, would you say anything that you *knew* would get you fired? Probably not. Now, if the only way you could keep that job were to lie to people on a regular basis, would you do that? Imagine the kind of person who would. If their actions on average are any measure, that's the kind of people you have representing you in Congress. They probably weren't that way when they arrived there. Like frogs sitting in a pot of slowly heating water, the money, the power, the lifestyle, and the social status corrupted them. If you and I were to acquire all of those things for basically sitting and talking, occasionally casting a vote, and then going on long vacations, who's to say how many of us wouldn't wind up same way. I'm sure there are congressmen and senators who really care about our country, but in the end they are outnumbered by those who care about their own wealth, power, and their own ideology just a little bit more.

That kind of money and power; the limousines and White House dinner parties, the bribes from lobbyists and free jet travel gradually change the way a person thinks. I'll give you a couple of examples.

If an *aeronautical engineer* sits down to design a new airplane, he'll ask himself questions like these: How many people will it carry, and over what distance, at what altitude, and at what speed? What type and shape of airfoil and wing configuration would be most efficient aerodynamically? What kind of engines, turboprop, turbofan or turbojet, would be most fuel-efficient? If a *politician* were to sit down to design a new airplane, he would ask himself *one* question: *What is going to get me re-elected, and increase my power and wealth?*

If a *structural engineer* is going to sit down and design a new highway, he would ask himself question like these: What kind of vehicles will it carry, and in what numbers? What speed will they be traveling? What kind of terrain is it going to be built over in terms of substrata and bedrock? Are there any mountains, hills or rivers to be crossed? What materials will last longest and be easiest to maintain? If a *politician* were to sit down to design the same highway, he or she would ask themselves *one* question: *What is going to get me re-elected and increase my power and wealth?*

Consider this: That aeronautical engineer, that structural engineer, the pilot of that new plane, the truck drivers on that new highway, doctors, nurses, lawyers, electricians, architects, beauticians, dog groomers and sixteen year old kids with cars all have one thing in common; they have to pass a test and carry a license that proves they know what they're doing. All a politician *ever* has to do is *get you to vote for them!*

I'm not discounting the fact that there have been extraordinary leaders in our government; men like George Washington, Thomas Jefferson, Abraham Lincoln, John Kennedy and Ronald Reagan and Trey Gowdy. If you'd like to see the signatures of fifty six more, all you have to do is look at the Declaration of Independence. The framers of the Constitution were also such men. (Incidentally, I highly recommend reading the Constitution. It is a little difficult because it's written in 18th Century English, but it still only took me about an hour, and several times I found myself saying "So *that's* where that comes from!" You can get a free copy of both the Declaration of Independence and the Constitution at www.Heritage.org.) Unfortunately, with the exception of Mr. Gowdy, all of those men also have one thing in common; they're all dead and they can't help us now.

And now on to the second thing that irked me about the radio commercial I heard back in Grand Junction. The Statement "Our world is getting so dangerous we can hardly afford to sleep, and it's only going to get worse for our children." Does anyone really believe that? Even if you take it as an exaggeration, is the world getting more dangerous every day? Drugs, guns, gangs, child molesters, and sexual predators are everywhere. Cell phones, high-tension power lines, nuclear power plants and oil spills threaten all of us every day. There are all kinds of horrible ways to die that people never had to worry about in the past. The past was so much safer, right?

Well, let's take a look at that. It's true that people in the past didn't have to worry about dying in car accidents, or plane crashes, or nuclear power plant explosions, or at the hands of machine gun toting drug dealers. No, they had to worry about dying in mining accidents, oxcart roll-overs, wild animal attacks, industrial fires, logging accidents, from contagious diseases, or in weather induced famines. If you go back far enough, they had to worry about Indian attacks, shipwrecks and the Black Plague. Go back even farther, and they had to worry about getting mauled by a wooly rhinoceros or getting eaten by a sabre toothed tiger. I've got a news flash for you: *The world has always been a dangerous place.* There have *always* been murderers. There have *always* been child molesters. There have *always* been criminals. There have **not** always been wooly rhinoceroses and sabre toothed cats.

Are there *more* murderers today? Of course. Are there *more* child molesters than there used to be? You bet'cha. Are *more* people dying in accidents? Absolutely! Why? Because there are *more people now;* a *lot* more. If the number of people doubles, so does the number among them who do bad things, but the per capita prevalence of those bad things does *not* increase. Are there more tornadoes, hurricanes, earthquakes, and tsunamis than there used to be? No, there are not. Why do we hear more about them? Weather satellites, and instant, worldwide telecommunications. You have to remember that prior to the beginning of the 20th century, the world moved at the speed of a walking horse. You didn't know about a hurricane until it clobbered someone, and then the news could take months to travel around the world instead of seconds. If it happened in an area where no one lived, you would never hear about it at all.

When the Internet came along, the pace quickened yet again. Forget about something being on the evening news tonight, it'll be on YouTube in 15 minutes. Another reason we hear more about natural disasters is that more people are moving into the areas where they occur; mainly ocean coastlines

So why does the world *seem* so much more dangerous today? Because there are people who get paid a lot of money to tell you that the world is more dangerous, and it's astounding how much we believe for no other reason than it is put in front of our faces on the evening news.

What a lot of people don't realize is that the news is not a public service. Do you see commercials on the news each night? There you go; it's a *commercial enterprise.* They don't keep you informed out of the goodness of their hearts, they make money by keeping you watching. The businesses that buy commercial time on your local stations do it to get their product out in front of the public. Some companies sponsor sports, some sponsor fictional dramas, some sponsor reality shows, and *some sponsor the news.* Their choices are influenced by who is going to be watching and what they're trying to sell. The more people watch the news, the more they are exposed to the commercials, the more of the sponsor's product they buy and the more money the sponsor makes. The news, like the rest of television is an advertising medium. It's as simple as that. The goal of the television stations is to get as many people watching their programs as possible. They make sports as exciting as possible. They make dramas as compelling as possible. They make reality shows as "Stab your buddy in the back and think you're someone important for it" as possible. (Sorry I just couldn't resist. Someday there will be a reality show called "Big Room With a Pile of Money and a Bunch of Sharp Knives.") They make science and nature shows as interesting as possible, and with the news, they make it as bleak as possible.

For some reason, people don't want to hear good news. Good news is boring. No one wants to hear about the air getting cleaner, which it has. They don't want to hear that there are more polar bears now than they were 50 years ago, which there are. If you put on a news program that showed only good news, the sponsors would lose money because no one would watch. People want to hear about murder, rape, and robbery. They want to hear about earthquakes, tornadoes, and hurricanes. They want to hear about death, destruction and doom. So is it any surprise that the TV news, in an effort to sell as much of their sponsors product as possible, gives us *more* of what we want? People in the TV news biz have a phrase for it: "If it bleeds, it leads!"

The problem is habituation. When any animal is exposed to any stimulus repeatedly, its response to that stimulus diminishes over time. It's how our nervous systems are wired and it happens all the time with every animal. It is why most people don't watch the same episode of the same television program over and over again, or read one book again and again to the exclusion of all others. It's why we don't like eating the same food every day. There is a definite evolutionary imperative to habituation. It keeps our brains from being overloaded with old data to the exclusion of new. If we keep reacting to that woolly mammoth way over there, we *won't* notice that much nearer Sabre-toothed tiger creeping up on us from right over *there.*

When the nightly news gives us embezzlement, we get used to it; it becomes blasé and we lose interest. We change the channel and we don't see the sponsor's commercials. We don't buy as much of their project, and they pull the commercials from the News Hour and put them someplace else. Advertising revenues at the station fall, and that's bad.

So the news department ups the ante. They graduate from embezzlement to robbery. Soon, we're going to get bored with robbery, and they have to escalate to rape. When rape can no longer hold our attention, they move up to murder. As we become more and more desensitized to what they're showing us, they have to keep giving us worse and worse things to keep us watching and keep their ad money coming in. Soon it's not enough to tell us the bad news, they have to show it to us. There was a time not so long ago when it would've been unthinkable to show a person plunging to their death over Niagara Falls, and yet I watched just such a report. A cameraman just happened to be on location filming something else when a man decided to commit suicide at the same location. Granted, he jumped in the river himself; no one pushed him, but it was still very disturbing to actually see the expression on his face as he disappeared over the edge. Even the newscast's anchorman was clearly uncomfortable, but the station aired the footage anyway. I've heard news reports that I purposely didn't pass on to anyone because they were so horrible I honestly don't believe anyone *needed* to know them. That's what the news has been reduced to these days.

Mark Twain once said "There are three kinds of lies: lies, damn lies, and statistics." How often do you think the news media manipulates statistics to make things sound *better* than they are? You can make statistics say anything. One of my favorite examples comes from a radio host named Mike McConnell, who broadcasts from AM 700 WLW in Cincinnati (or at lest he did when I first wrote this. I hope he's still there.) The basic theme of Mike's show is common sense, and he dishes it out mercilessly. Needless to say he drives a lot of people crazy. One day in the summer of 2008, he discussed a bill being considered in the California State Legislature which would outlaw cell phone use while driving. The lawmakers cited a study finding that cell phone related car accidents had increased dramatically over the last few years. Certainly sounds like an open and shut case, doesn't it? But does it mean that cell phones *caused* the increase in accidents, or does it mean that since many more people own cell phones, more of them just happened to be talking on the cell phones when they become involved in accidents they would've had anyway? The fact is that during the same period of time, the *overall* accident rate had been decreasing. In other words, the more people used cell phones while driving, the fewer accidents there were. Of course, this doesn't mean that cell phone use while driving *prevents* accidents. No doubt many accidents are caused in exactly that way. The point is, post hoc ergo proctor hoc (after, and therefore because of) reasoning is not a sufficient basis for making public policy. Mike suggested that the California legislature ought to look into anti-lock brake related accidents. If you did the research, you would probably find that the number of accidents that happened while drivers are applying their anti-lock brakes has increased dramatically over the last 30 years. (Of course, there are dramatically more cars *equipped with* anti-lock brakes over the last 30 years, but we won't bother the politicians with that.) Therefore using the logic of a "B follows A, and therefore A causes B", we must conclude that anti-lock brakes cause accidents, and should be outlawed. Once again just because you're in government doesn't mean you're smart.

Both politicians and the television news tell you about all the worst things that are going on, all the most unfortunate things that have happened and the worst side of human nature, without all that pesky hope and optimism. If most of us get our news from the television, it's no wonder that we think the world is going to Hell in a hand basket. According to the television news, the world is one big inner city.

It isn't.

There are still thousands of places in this country where people have respect for human life, look out for their neighbors, and exhibit the best in human character. In many of these places, people still don't routinely lock their doors. What are these places? They're called "Small Towns" and there are a heck of a lot more than there are inner cities.

I'm not telling you to throw caution to the wind and stop taking common sense precautions for your own safety or that of your loved ones. I'm just asking you to take what you hear with a grain of salt, and if it's being financed by commercial sponsors, make it a pinch. I'm just saying the notion that your fellow human being is more and more dire a threat to you with each passing day is ludicrous, and completely unsupportable by actual evidence. I have no idea why people do not like to hear good news, but it doesn't seem like that is going to change. The good news is a little harder to track down, but it's well worth the effort.

Corporate Greed

A few years ago while visiting my family in Colorado, I got into a lively discussion with my sister concerning all things political. A couple of times the discussion got lively enough that both my wife and my mother felt compelled to leave the room for a few moments, lest their own liveliness be taken out on my cranium or solar plexus, but once my sister and I got a feel for each other's debating style, we mostly had a rollicking good time.

As with any comparison of Conservatism versus Liberalism (That's what we considered ourselves at the time), we spent a certain amount of time on the subject of corporate greed, and why it is the reason so many American jobs are being shipped overseas to places like India and China. I suggested that if we lowered, or even eliminated the corporate income tax as has been done in places like Ireland, that not only would those companies come galloping back, but the rest of the free world would be hot on their heels, wanting to open manufacturing facilities and service centers and creating millions of jobs. My sister considered this for what must have been whole seconds before conceding that perhaps that was *part* of the problem, but the rest is **GREED!** Greedy right wing capitalist big-wigs putting hard-working Americans out on the streets and sending their jobs to foreign countries, where they exploit and oppress the masses by paying them a pittance compared to what they paid the Americans who used to do the same jobs, all the while raking in multiple millions of dollars and stuffing them into their own greedy pockets. It has to be greed, I tell you! It *has to be*! ***It has to!***

The thing was, I didn't have a good counter argument. The fact is, jobs *have* been going overseas, people in foreign countries *do* work for less than Americans, and there *are* corporate CEOs making millions of dollars. How could I justify anything that could be construed as doing a favor for such greedy people?

I had a lousy night's sleep that night, which meant my wife had a lousy night's sleep too, but I just could not turn my brain off. I just kept going over and over what my sister and said and how miserably I had failed to make my case. All I accomplished was to convince her that I was on the side of greed and exploitation.

By the morning I had it mostly figured out. While still lying in bed I asked my wife if she would be my sounding board. She declined. Later that morning I asked the same favor of my mother. Her reply was rolling eyes and "The Big Sigh." Evidently they were both still feeling some residual liveliness from the previous day's discussion. Would my sister listen to anything I had to say? She seemed very attached to the notion of greedy capitalists stuffing their pockets. The more I thought about it, the more she reminded me of global warming....uh, sorry, *climate change* activists. If you tell these people that "Hey, guess what? It turns out according to weather satellite measurements, the Earth's temperature has remained stable for the last 19 years, and according to the governments own scientists, Antarctica has actually been gaining billions of tons of ice every decade", you would think that would be good news to them. You'd think they would be relieved. Instead, their reaction is something more along the lines of: LIAR! LIAR! There *is* man-made global war.... there *is* man-made *climate change*! **There is! There is!** The similarity was uncanny. Clearly I had my work cut out for me.

The idea that corporate greed is responsible for the loss of American jobs and the exploitation of foreign workers depends on some interesting assumptions. One is that greed is a uniquely *American* trait. As I mentioned earlier, Ireland used to be one of the poorest countries in Europe. Then they lowered their corporate income tax rate to 9%, as opposed to our 39%, the second highest in the world. Corporations flooded into Ireland, building factories, putting people to work and producing goods and services. It's not only foreign corporations that are enjoying the lower tax rate there either; It's Irish corporations too. Are we to believe that there are no greedy capitalists in Ireland? It's certainly not the cheapest labor market in the world. People there are making good money, and there are plenty of people elsewhere in the world willing to work for less. So why are greedy Irish capitalists not causing Irish jobs to leave Ireland like rats leaving a sinking ship? The answer is simple, isn't it? It's only *American* capitalists who are greedy, right?

Another assumption is that American corporations are the only ones manufacturing the goods they produce and paying the wages they pay in the foreign countries to which they've relocated, and that the United States is the only place those goods are consumed. My sister likes to use the example of Levi Strauss, who's clothes used to be manufactured in America but are now made in India where they pay their workers a much lower wage.

Personally if we're going to discuss economics, I like to use the old College Economics 101 tool of widgets. I really do. I mean, everybody needs widgets don't they? So let's talk about the Liberty Bell Widget Company, which used to manufacture widgets in the U.S. but moved its last manufacturing facility to India in 1990, where they pay their workers exactly $2.00 per hour. What some people never consider is that the Hare Krishna Widget Company had been making widgets there for years before Liberty Bell ever showed up, and their Indian workers were perfectly happy to work for *them* for $1.00 per hour because it was better than anything else available to them. So now Liberty Bell comes to town, doubles the workers incomes, and somehow I'm supposed to believe that Liberty Bell is exploiting these people. I haven't figured out how doubling someone's standard of living is evil, but I'm working on it. I think it might be something like paying a homeless person $20 for wiping off your windshield at a stoplight. "What? I can't put a roof over my head for a measly twenty dollars! You evil bastard!"

Whether you like it or not, whether it's fair or not, the world is now a global marketplace, and unless you want to re-institute isolationism and ban all imports to the United States from the rest of the world, then American companies like Liberty Bell, paying high corporate taxes, complying with ever increasing government regulation, and paying their employees high wages have to compete with companies like the Hare Krishna Widget Company, who pay lower corporate taxes, are not regulated nearly as much, pay their employees lower wages, and by they way, also export their widgets to this country, where they sit of the shelves right next to Liberty Bell Widgets. On that playing field, who do you expect to win? Who do you *want* to win?

Another assumption is that greed is a very recent phenomenon. Every job that moved overseas used to be here, right up until the time it left. Liberty Bell Widgets packed up shop and moved overseas in 1990. That means they were *here* until then. Are we to believe that their greed did not exist before 1990? How about the 1980s, when America was in the middle of the longest economic expansion in the history of the world? Were there no greedy Capitalists then? How about in the 1950's? No greed then? No cheap foreign labor then? How about the late 1800s when the Rockefellers, the Vanderbilts and the Duponts were amassing their fortunes? Am I supposed to believe there was no such thing as greed in the Gilded Age, and that there was no one in the world willing to work for less than Americans earned at that time? If greed and cheap labor are the main ingredients for jobs moving overseas, and those two things have always existed, then why were the jobs *ever* here? And yet, they were. So the question is, what happened in the 1990s to change the equation?

Perhaps the 90s was a time when hundreds of companies across the United States were simultaneously taken over by singularly greedy boards of directors, who threw out the benevolent former management, transferred ownership of all their stock to greedy stockholders, and proceeded to fire Americans and send their jobs to foreign countries so that they could all stuff more money into their own pockets.

Or, perhaps the 90s was the decade when hundreds of thousands of members of corporate America, who only a few years before *had been* caring benefactors of their employees and moral stewards of their companies assets and responsibilities, simultaneously became infected with evil, threw away their moral compasses and proceeded to fire Americans and send their jobs to foreign countries so that they could all stuff more money into their own pockets.

I'll tell you now that my sister, like a lot of people, didn't realize that corporations don't pay taxes. They never have and never will, they only *collect* them.....from *you*! Any corporate tax increase is passed on to the consumer in the form of higher prices for their goods or services. She was incredulous. She reasoned that if they didn't even *pay* taxes, then why should *we* care how high they are? Excuse me, maybe I should say that again: Because *they* don't pay the corporate income taxes, **you do**! The government passes a new tax to punish evil corporations for making obscene windfall profits, and it comes out of *your* pocket! Does this make you happy? Do you think this is right and just?

Here's another excellent example of what people fail to take into account. Let's look at oil companies. Yes, they made record billions of dollars in profits in the last few years. They also *spent* record billions of dollars in order to do it. The important question is not what was their profit, but what was their *profit margin*? (Incidentally, if you don't know the difference between a *profit* and a *profit margin,* get the heck out of here and don't come back until you do, because right now, you are not qualified to participate in any serious discussion about economics. I'm serious. Go, learn, return.) The answer is the same as it has been for a long, long time; about ten cents per gallon.

Now, here comes the government to your rescue, determined to punish those greedy oil companies for vacuuming out your wallet. They tax the oil companies twenty cents per gallon. That'll show'em! Twenty cents doesn't sound like all that much, does it? Except that if you expect the oil companies to pay the tax *without* raising their prices, you have eliminated 100% of their profits and then some. They can either eat the new tax and go bankrupt, in which case, no one has any gasoline to fuel their cars and the corporations employees are now unemployed, *or*, they can raise the price of their gas by twenty cents. Which of these alternatives would *you* choose in their place?

Anyhow, it's important to know that in order to understand the explanation I'd like to offer for the current situation. I propose that for the Liberty Bell Widget Company, 1990 was not the beginning of a process, but the culmination of one. That was the year when the cost of high corporate taxes and the cost of complying with an ever increasing burden of government regulation, passed on to the consumer in higher prices, finally made Liberty Bell Unable to compete with the Hare Krishna Widget Company. Liberty Bell widgets became so expensive that people started buying Hare Krishna widgets instead. Remember, Hare Krishna pays it's employees half as much as Liberty Bell, but they don't even have to sell them for *half* as much to corner the market, all they have to do is sell them for *less* than Liberty Bell.

My sister thinks those job should've been kept in this country. I agree, but what would it have taken to do that? When the corporate taxes and government red tape kept increasing, Liberty Bell could've refrained from doing what every other corporation has always done. They could've kept the jobs here, kept the wages high and paid the increased taxes out of their profits. Of course, that would only work until their profits dwindled down to zero, went negative and the company went bankrupt, ceased to exist, destroyed the wealth of its stockholders, threw all of its employees out of work, and sucked untold millions of dollars out of the American economy. That solution doesn't work very well, does it?

Okay, how about this: As the corporate taxes kept increasing, Liberty Bell could have kept the jobs here, kept some kind of profit margin, and simply paid the increased taxes by continuing to lower wages. Of course, *that* would only work until the wages became so low that no one would work for them any longer, and Liberty Bell went bankrupt, ceased to exist, destroyed the wealth of its stockholders, threw all of it's employees out of work, and sucked untold millions of dollars out of the American economy. Somehow *that* solution doesn't seem that much better. I have to wonder, if Liberty Bell Widgets had tried either one of *these* solutions would they still be blamed for the loss of those jobs?

Another possible solution would be to refuse to pay the higher taxes and refuse to comply with the increasing government regulations. Let me know how *that* one works out.

The hard truth is, the money to pay the taxes and comply with the regulations has to come from somewhere. Rather than trying any of the previous solutions, none of which would have worked in the long run, Liberty Bell made a tough choice that would; they found a cheaper labor market that would save them enough money to pay their taxes without destroying the wealth of their stockholders, without going bankrupt and ceasing to exist as a company, and incidentally, without throwing all the people *still* employed by their distribution network in the United States out of work. Those evil, greedy sons of bitches!

So there you have three possible explanations for the current situation. I'll leave it to you to decide which one is more plausible. It is my humble opinion that what American companies like Liberty Bell have done is not greed, but survival.

But just for the sake of argument…. let's say it *is* greed. If greed motivated companies to send jobs abroad, then instead of continuing to do the same things that motivated them to do that, why not use *greed* to get them back? As we said before, the very fact that they *left* here means that they used to *be* here. And why were they here in the first place? Because up until the day they left, they could make more money here than they could there. It's the only explanation their greed would have allowed. So why not re-create the business conditions back then? First, get rid of unnecessary regulations (and before your head explodes, notice I said *unnecessary* regulations, not *all* regulations. Regulations to keep people safe are one thing, but we acquire thousands and thousands of new pages of them *every year*, and each one of them can cost from thousands to millions of dollars to comply with, *every year*. We have regulations about the amount of lima beans school children may be served in a week. We have regulations that dictate the exact height of handrails in stairwells to the half-inch. We have regulations that require monks to be licensed funeral directors. We have regulations requiring computer technicians to obtain private investigator's licenses. We have regulations prohibiting rescuing whales without proper credentials. Do you honestly believe we need *every one* of these?) If you wonder where the ridiculous regulations come from, I'll tell you a little bit more about that later.

Next, lower our corporate tax rate to below that of the countries that now have the jobs. While we're at it, lower it to zero. After all if they don't even *pay* the taxes why should *you* care how *low* they are? (Hint: because it puts more money back in your pocket, that's why.)

Without the crushing burden of the second highest corporate tax rate in the world and the cost of complying with tens of thousands of pages of regulations, the corporations would then have two choices. They could stay in the foreign countries and pay their higher taxes, or they could come back here, pay no taxes, undercut the price of their foreign competitors and be king of the hill again. Now I ask you, what would their *greed* dictate they do?

So there you have three explanations and *five* possible solutions. Once again, I'll leave it to you to decide which rings true. Personally, I think my explanation and the last two solutions make the most sense, except for one pesky little thing; that greedy American capitalist with the 5 million dollar bonus that he doesn't need and therefore presumably doesn't deserve. You thought I forgot about him, didn't you? Well I didn't. Let's talk about him.

You can go back-and-forth all day long about whether or not he earned it or deserves it, but what I want to ask you is, what does he *do* with that money? Do you think he stuffs it into a big fishbowl and sits at his dining room table at night with his arms around it, laughing maniacally and shouting "It's mine, *all mine?*" If he does that, it's never going to be any more than 5 million, and inflation will gradually make it worth less and less.

Do you think he blows every penny of it on huge mansions, airplanes, diamond rings and caviar, and that he has no stock portfolio and fifty bucks in the bank? Just about everything he owns with the exception of the house is guaranteed to depreciate, making his net worth less and less as time goes by. Does that sound like what a truly greedy man would do?

As a matter of fact, he *did* buy an airplane; a really nice one. He bought a Gulfstream V. It's practically an airliner. Here's the interesting thing about that: Someone had to manufacture it, and that included buying parts, components and materials from people who had to manufacture *them,* who bought their raw materials from still other people who ultimately had to mine the natural resources out of the ground. Someone had to sell it to him, someone has to maintain it, someone has to fuel it, someone has to manufacture the fuel, someone has to crew it and someone has to cater it. Someone has to keep track of it on radar and keep it from bumping into other planes as it flies through the sky. That *one jet* could easily represent dozens of good paying jobs for Americans. Now multiply that by all the private jets in America. If he also bought a yacht, the same principle would apply to it.

After he buys the jet and the boat, and maybe even an American made car (that someone had to manufacture, sell, maintain, fuel…. you get my drift) he could decide to increase his wealth even further by reinvesting in his own company, expanding his operations and in creating even more jobs for people like you and me. Or, he could invest in a new start up company that could be the next Apple or Microsoft, and could eventually employee thousands of people, allowing them to provide a good life for their families, and with their everyday spending on food, clothing, and consumer goods, put millions more dollars *into* the economy.

If he does nothing more than put the money in a bank, it is now available for an education loan for a young woman to go to college, so that she won't be stuck in a dead-end job for the rest of her life. It's available for a car loan for a man who has just landed a really good job that could finally allow his family to get ahead, but it's in a different city, so he needs a reliable car to get back-and-forth. It's available for a home loan for young couple to buy their first house, and begin to build their own nest egg through its appreciation.

He *could* do those things with that money, but he'll never get the chance, because once again your government is going to step in and avenge you of that capitalist's greed. They're going to take it, either with a highly progressive income tax or by forcing him to buy carbon credits, or if some people had their way, just flat out telling him he's not allowed to make that much. No matter how they do it, they are determined to confiscate his ill-gotten millions. It will disappear into the black hole of government and it will be gone, vanished, end of story.

So now, that start up company will never get off the ground. The young entrepreneur who wanted to start it never will, because the capital wasn't there. He will just keep slogging away for his current employer. All the jobs he could've created will never exist, and neither will all the money his employees would have put into the economy. That young woman won't get that education loan, because the capital just wasn't there. She won't go back to school, and will be stuck in the dead-end job for who knows how long. That family man won't to get the car loan, because the capital wasn't there. He'll lose that job he just landed, and have to see if he can get his old one back. That young couple won't get their home loan, because the capital wasn't there, and they'll have to continue paying rent on an apartment that will cost them thousands of dollars every year and never earn them a single penny's equity. Jobs never exist, ambitions are stifled, and dreams are crushed. But you know what? All of that really is okay, because that capitalist was *greedy*, and he **didn't deserve** that money.

True Free-Market Capitalist economies are just like trees. Leave them alone, and they grow, they expand, they branch out, and fruit pops out all over them. Cut off a branch, and any fruit it would have borne beyond the cut will never be. Cut it off close enough to the trunk and you will kill the whole tree.

True Free Market Capitalism is the surest path to prosperity for the most people. It leaves prosperity in its wake everywhere it goes, *as long as it's allowed to*. The rest of the world knows this. Countries like China and Cuba are moving *toward* capitalism, and prospering every step of the way, while *our* country is moving *away* from it. Governments can take actions that grow economies or shrink them. The action that makes a functioning economy *grow* consists mainly of getting the hell out of the way. Some taxation is inevitable, but it is a necessary evil. Corporate taxes serve no other purpose than to punish those who produce, and the government can't even seem to get that right. The only people they end up punishing is us.

Are there businessman who are just plain greedy? Of course there are, but let me ask you this: are they going to use the highest quality materials, or the cheapest they can find? Are they going to hire the best and most qualified workers, or the cheapest they can find? And, are they going to charge a reasonable price for their goods, or as much as they can possibly get? Genuinely greedy businessmen tend to produce shoddy, overpriced products. How long do you think they will last in a truly free marketplace where they must compete with the best mankind has to offer?

Some people believe that the only thing a "Free Market" means is that greedy businessmen (and women) are free to screw you over any way they like, and there's not a damn thing anyone can do to stop them. There are a lot of people who would dearly love for you to believe that. They've been telling you that for 150 years. That's…. well, how can I put this delicately and in a way that won't offend anyone…. oh yes, that's a *lie*. The people who are going to do something about it are you and me, because a *real* Free Market is free on *both sides* of the sales counter. (I'd like you to repeat that last sentence three times to yourself. If you think it's a lie after you've read the next paragraph, I'd love to hear your explanation of why.)

You see, shortly after a greedy businessman decides to separate you from your money, another businessman is going to notice that he's ripping you off and you don't like getting ripped off. It makes you really miffed. He knows that if he gives you a better product, with better service, at a lower price, *he's* going to get your business instead, so that's exactly what he does and that's exactly what happens. His *self-interested* decision to grab a bigger share of the market gives you a better choice, and your *self-interested* decision to take the alternative has left the both of you wealthier, happier and better off. Incidentally, your combined decisions also put that greedy businessman out of business, and now there's not a damn thing *he* can do about it.

On second thought, that's not exactly true. There are actually two things he could do about it. His first alternative is to do exactly what his rival businessman did, and find a way to give you an even better product, with even better service at an even lower price. He gets your business back and once again leaves the both of you better off than you were before.

His second alternative is to go buy himself some politicians, who can do two things for him. First, they can pass a law saying that you no longer have a choice. (Think health insurance here: hundreds of companies, two or three choices for you, courtesy of the government.) They may even give him an exclusive contract to provide you with the choice they've made for you. They do this with the best of intentions. They sincerely want to help you and give you "justice" in the face of those evil greedy bastards. They feel compelled to take action on your behalf because they also sincerely believe that you're not smart enough to solve your own problems, and they are.

Another payoff they can provide that businessman for buying them is passing thousands of pages of new regulations. They will ostensibly be for your safety. (Remember, if that handrail is half an inch too low, it could be the difference between life and death!) What they are *actually* designed to do is make it more difficult, or, even impossible, if they are expensive enough to comply with, for any new competitors to enter the market, because only the big established corporations have pockets deep enough to pay for complying with them. So what ends up happening is, *politicians* have decided that **this** guy will win, and **that** guy will lose, not because *that* guy is producing a dangerous product, or engaging in unethical business practices, or even because he's a bad person, but because **this** guy has enough money to *buy* himself a **[expletive deleted]** politician!

Now that the government has become involved, there really isn't a damn thing you can do about it. Now, it doesn't matter how shoddy a product is put in front of you. You have no choice but to accept and pay for it.

*This is **not** Free Market Capitalism.* Regulations to keep people safe are one thing, but the second a bureaucrat, at a politician's behest, writes a regulation, whether as a payoff for huge campaign contributions or for lots of lobbyist schmoozing, that does not ensure someone's safety but instead favors one business entity over another, *you no longer have a free market;* you have a *government controlled* market. This is a system known as Crony Capitalism, or as Free Market Capitalists such as myself like to abbreviate it, *Crapitalism. Without turning to the government and bribing them to use the force of law, greedy businessmen would have no power whatsoever to make you do anything.*

So I have to ask: Who is *really* the problem, greedy businessmen, or the government?

I've had this conversation with several people who would call themselves liberals. They followed my reasoning up to this point, even questioning some of their lifelong assumptions about Capitalism. I was convinced that I was on the verge of actually changing their minds when something fascinating happened. It was at this very point that those minds, like rubber bands that had been stretched too far, suddenly **snapped** back to their original shape, and they doubled down on their previous positions, *insisting* that the problem is still greedy, unprincipled people ***forcing*** us to buy overpriced products we don't want, ***forcing*** us to make decisions that are against our best interests, ***destroying*** our environment and our society, ***denying*** us the choices that will better our lives. Okay, then my question is this: How do they do it?

How do they do it?

Do they bombard the population with powerful mind control rays from huge transmitters, strategically placed throughout the country? You and I both know that technology doesn't exist. Do they dig up dirt on every single consumer in America and then use it to blackmail them? Have you ever had your phone right in the middle of the night, and when you answered it, heard a voice say "This is Wal-Mart. You'd better start buying our crap, or we'll spill the beans on you." Do they put up roadblocks, herding traffic on the road into their parking lots? In all my life, I've never run into such a roadblock. Do they post armed thugs with guns and knives at the front door of their competitor's stores to deny you entry? I've never spoken with anyone who had that kind of deadly force used on them, ever.

So *how* do they *do* it?

The truth is, there is only one entity on the face of this planet that can *force* hundreds of millions of people to behave in any particular way, and *it ain't Walmart or Monsanto!* It is to *that* entity that greedy, unprincipled people *must* turn if they are to have any influence over you whatsoever. It is their *only* option if they are to achieve the goals you ascribe to them. Without bribing that entity; keeping it in their pocket to use as a tool to accomplish their aims, they are completely, totally, powerless.

So if greed is utterly powerless *until you add the ingredient of government*, how on earth is the answer *more government?*

Some people will say that we have to have the government involved; that without direct government oversight at all times, corporations will immediately start operating with such total disregard for the welfare of the consumers that people cold wind up dead! Several years ago, the Tyson Corporation petitioned the FDA for the right to self inspect their chicken processing plants. A young relative of mine stated on social media that "This obviously proves that they don't care about consumers", the implications being that without the government overseeing the sanitation of their facilities, they would immediately cease to maintain their cleanliness, they would produce a toxic product, and their customers would get sick and possibly even die.

If their customers get sick and die, *who's going to buy their chicken?*

Lets say for just a moment that the FDA granted Tyson's request, and what my young relative's implied prediction came true; that some consumers became very sick due to Tyson's "not caring about them." Here's a few questions for her: In this day and age, do you think those sick consumers are more likely to:

A: Suffer in silence.

Or,

B: Get on Facebook, Twitter, YouTube, Instagram and half a dozen other social media outlets, and make damn sure that by tomorrow morning, half a billion people will know about Tyson's treachery? *Which do you think is **more** likely?*

Upon hearing of what an uncaring, unethical, evil, greedy bunch of scumbags every one of Tyson's employees are, are those half a billion people more likely to:

A: Say "Hey, I better sign up for some of *that?"*

Or,

Avoid Tyson chicken like the plague, pass the word on to even more people, and put a serious dent in Tyson's profits, maybe even putting them out of business? *Which do you think is **more** likely?*

And if you and I know these things, don't you think the board of directors of Tyson know them too?

Do truly greedy people want to make as much money as they can for a very *short* time, or a very *long* time? Are truly unethical people more likely to invest billions of dollars in infrastructure to get the fleeting profits they'll rake in in that short span of time before their lack of ethics and principles catch up with them, or are they more likely to do everything they can to make sure their customers are healthy and happy with their product, and keep coming back to buy it for year after year? Isn't it in the interest of their greed to maintain the cleanest, safest facilities they can? If they really do want to make as much money as they can for as long as they can, how is the force of government going to be any more effective than the forces of the Free Market, in which they *have no other choice* but to satisfy their customers or perish?

The most accurate and inspiring definition of Free Market Capitalism I've ever come across comes from a book called The Morality of Capitalism, by Tom G. Palmer. Free Market Capitalism is: *"A system of production and exchange that is based on the rule of law, on equality of rights for all, on the freedom to trade, on the freedom to innovate, on the guiding discipline of profits and losses, and on the right to enjoy the fruits of one's labor, of one's savings, and one's investments without fearing confiscation or restriction from those who have invested not in production of wealth, but in political power."* Crony Capitalists hate Free Market Capitalism as much as Socialists do, because it affords no special privileges to anyone, wealthy or not.

Now I have a couple of questions for you. Which of these forces do you think is more likely to have brought us to where we are now, the free market, or government? Competition in a *free* market increases quality, decreases price and increases availability for all people, at every income level, every single time. (If you want an example of this, look at cell phones. Forty years ago, a mobile phone was the size of a brick and cost $4,000.00. Now, most *poor* people have one.) You can denounce that as Capitalist propaganda until you're blue in the face, and when you have no breath left, it will still be true. Anything you can cite as a failure of the Free Market can be demonstrated in less than 30 seconds to be a direct result of *government interference* in the free market.

The CEOs of big corporations make a lot of money, but they make it by producing products and services that people need and want, and in the process they employ millions of people. The fact is, in this country it is virtually impossible to get rich *without helping* a lot of people. (Yes, I know there's Bernie Madoff, but just look at where he is now.) Our government should not be making it more difficult for that to be done here, and easier for it to be done someplace else, and proposals like current President-elect Donald Trump's to fine corporations for sending jobs overseas is just piling one failed government intervention on top of another.

For a government to control the economy under the guise of "making things fair" takes a concerted and ongoing political effort to get poor people to hate rich people enough to mean them harm. For Capitalism to spontaneously spring into existence requires only two pre-existing ingredients: a monetary exchange system....

....and *freedom.*

Think about that.

I vote freedom.

Minimum Wage

Wendy's, the giant hamburger chain announced recently that they are going to start putting automated ordering kiosks in some of their restaurants. This was of course followed by immediate outrage from people across the nation who accused Wendy's of taking this action to avoid paying their employees what they're worth, which is evidently $15.00 per hour these days.

And of course, there was plenty of chatter about it on social media, especially with this being an election year. I made the mistake of replying to a post on Facebook on this subject, and was immediately given the what for by a charming gentleman who made sure I knew that he is a successful business owner (and a veteran, and a minority, though what that has to do with anything I have not yet figured out.) He claimed that automation is just a fact of modern life, and the Wendy's employees displaced by the automated kiosks will simply re-train for other jobs within the company. Problem solved.

How is that going to work? If the whole Idea behind the automation is to save labor costs (and it is), How is Wendy's going to do that if they keep all those employees? Before, they had the labor costs for those employees. If they *keep* those employees around after the automation, then they have the cost of upgrading to automation, *plus* the cost of paying all those employees $15.00 and hour (if you raise the minimum wage that that amount), *plus* the cost of retraining all of them. How have they saved any money? Why did they automate? The truth is, they are not going to keep those employees, they are going to lay them off. So how is the higher minimum wage supposed to help them if they have no jobs?

The consensus seems to be that big corporations like Wendy's should just stop being so greedy and just take some of those obscene profits they rake in every year and stuff into their pockets, and pay their employees $15.00 an hour. That is the obvious and logical way to attack this problem, and it *would* attack it.....

....exactly 0.3% of it.

Here's what a lot of people don't know: Huge corporations like Wendy's constitute only 0.3% of all the employers in America. Anther 10.1% of them are companies with fewer than 500 employees. *The remaining 89.6% of them are companies with 20 or fewer employees.* Most people don't know *this* either: The average salary of a small business owner (at least the half of them who actually pay themselves a regular salary) in 2012 was **$68,000 a year**, and that's actually about $4,000 less than it was just the year before. The vast majority of employers who are going to be impacted by a $15.00 minimum wage (yeah, I think 90% counts as a vast majority) are business owners with twenty or fewer employees making around $68,000 a year, so if your going to talk about how a $15.00 minimum wage will affect the economy as a whole, you have to talk about *them.* Very few of them are multi-millionaires, and as a rule they don't have enough money to buy robots to work for them.

I'm going to start using some numbers here. I'll tell you right now that I haven't computed each one to the penny. I'm not a mathematician and chances are neither are you. I'm talking about ideas here. I'm talking about concepts that hold true whether you do the math or not. If you want that kind of detail, I have a very good friend who is an accomplished mathematician. He even worked as an actuary for several years. I'm not him. Here we go.

Now lets consider that that small businessman has living expenses just like everyone else. Let's say he lives really cheaply, and I mean *really* cheaply on $20,000 year, so he has a discretionary income of $48,000 a year. If he pays each of his twenty employees the current federal minimum wage of $7.25 and hour, he's paying them a total of $301,600.00 per year. Now, you want him to pay them more than twice that much ($624,000.00).

So you're asking a guy with $48,000.00 to spare to come up with another $322.400.00 to pay his employees for doing no more work than they're doing now. Where is he supposed to get it? If you multiply that by the 5,730,000 similarly sized small businesses in America, you're demanding that an amount of money so big that my smartphone calculator can't even handle it to magically appear out of nowhere.

How is that supposed to happen?

The money to pay everyone $15.00 and hour does not suddenly and magically spring into existence just because someone says it ought to. It has to be *created!* So how does that happen? Money is a medium of exchange. The dollar bill you hold in your hand is actually nothing more than a *tangible symbol of value*. So where did the value come from?

Lets say there is a big pool of oil a mile below the Badlands of North Dakota, which in fact, there is. You don't own the land it's under and I'm not offering to sell it to you, I'm just *telling* you it's there. So how much monetary value does that knowledge have to you? How much money will you pay me just to know that oil is down there? If you're a fairly intelligent person, the answer is nothing. If it's something more than that, hey let's talk!

Now, *turn that oil into gasoline, and bring it to where you are,* and suddenly it *does* have value to you. It's something for which you're willing to pay a specific dollar amount right now. So what happened in between that turned something worth nothing into something worth cash?

Another example. You drive up to a McDonalds and peek in the window, and you see the place is deserted; not a person in sight, just frozen bags of hamburger patties and French fries sitting on the counters inside. How much value do those frozen bags have to you? How much will you pay to peek in that window? Again, if you're smart, it's nothing, *but,* hand a bag with a nice hot double cheeseburger and some crispy French fries in it out the drive though window, and suddenly it has value to you.

So in both of these examples, what happened that turned something that was worthless into something that has a definite quantifiable value? What happened was people, drilling and pumping that oil out of the ground and refining it into gasoline and transporting it across the country. What happened was the people in that McDonalds frying up those burgers and French fries and putting them in those bags. The truth is, **the only thing that creates value is the labor of people.** There is not a single product or service on the face of the earth that does not involve people working away for eight hours a day, or 12 hours a day, or 14 hours a day (I had that job once; 14 hours a night, 5 nights a week.)

Now the next big question is, **how much** value does all those people's labor create? Well, that depends....how much will *you* pay for that double cheeseburger and fries? Fifty dollars? Nope! Thirty dollars? NOPE! Ten dollars? UH-UH!....

....*Five dollars?* YES! Okay, now let's inch the other way. $5.50? Yes. $5.75? Mmmmm, okay, but you're not entirely happy with it. There will quickly come a point where the price is the absolute limit of what you're willing to pay. That is the maximum value the cheeseburger and fries has to you. Well believe it or not, when you find the point where it is the maximum that *most* people are willing to pay, that is not only the value it has to you, *that is the value it has, period.* Take the price higher than that and some people will stop buying it. Take it much higher and a *lot* of people will stop buying it. Take it high enough and *no one* will buy it. So take it back down to where *most* people will buy it, and **that is the value of the product**, and it is directly tied to the amount of value added by the labor of the employees who produced it. *The value of any product or service is not determined by how much the person who produces it wanst to be paid for it, it's determined by how much the* **customer** *is willing to pay for it.*

So let me ask you this: Why should a small business owner sell you his product for *less* than its value? Why should he and his employees put all that value into his product with all their hard work, and then give it away to you? If he does that, then he *really is* not paying them what they're worth. I mean sure, it's good for you, but why exactly should he sacrifice his prosperity for your benefit and to his detriment, especially since it was he who took all the risk and responsibility and put all of his blood, sweat and tears into creating the company (and not insignificantly, creating all those jobs for all those people *you* now want to protect from him!)

The answer is, he shouldn't. Setting the price at the value is good for you (if it wasn't, you wouldn't pay it) **and** *it's good for him*. It is the price at which the *most good is being done for the most people*. So the price of any product naturally tends to be the maximum amount people are will to pay for that product, and that does not give the small business owner a lot of wiggle room. The money brought in by that price is all he has to work with when setting wages for his employees. In order for him to pay them higher wages, more value has to be added to the product, in order for the customers to be willing to pay more for it. If you force him to pay all of his employees more than twice as much for no more work than they're doing now, and no more value added to the product, you're demanding that he pull that extra money out of thin air, and he can't do that.

So if the minimum wage is more than doubled to $15.00, the small business owner has only three possibilities of how to handle it. One would be to take the extra money out of his profits. The problem with that solution is, most people think the average small business profit margin is 36% when it's actually somewhere around 3%. (That's right, the average small business owner makes around 3% profit, and you want him to raise wages *more than 100%*. At this point, we don't even need my mathematician friend.) They also think that all of that profit goes straight into the business owner's pocket. If it did that, it would be called his *salary*. Profit most often goes back into the business to expand it, which usually involves *more jobs*. Take away that profit, and you eliminate those jobs. Who have you helped then?

The second possibility is to raise the price of the product. You remember, the price that is naturally set near the maximum that most people are willing to pay, and if you raised it significantly, a lot of people will stop buying it? Well, you just raised it significantly! So how long do you think that 3% profit is going to last if *most people stop buying the product*. A huge number of businesses would promptly go under for lack of customers, throwing not only the business owner, but all of those very employees you wanted to help out of work. Not only that, but since everyone else had to raise *their* prices, all of those newly unemployed people now have to pay more for everything they buy. They're going to stop buying a lot of the things they used to buy, which means more businesses go under, which means even more people out of work, who won't be able to by the things *they* used to by, which means even more businesses going under.... and that, children, is how **depressions** get under way! How have you helped any of them?

Here's another thing to keep in mind. If you pay $10.00 dollars for something, you're getting $10.00 worth of value (again, if you weren't, you wouldn't buy it.) Doubling that price in order to pay doubled wages *does not magically double the value of the product!* If it's something you can do without, you're going to do without it. If it's something you cannot do without (food, water, shelter) then you'll continue to buy it, but it's *still only worth $10.00*, even though you're now paying $20.00 for it. So what has actually happened is, in passing a $15.00 minimum wage, the government is forcing you to hand over an extra $10.00 every time you buy that product, so that the business owner can pass it on to his workers, and there you have it, just another good ol' *Socialist redistribution of wealth,* which can *only* last until you run out of other people's money and there is no more wealth to be redistributed.

The only reality left for the small business owner is this: If he has enough money to pay *all* of his twenty employees $7.25 an hour, then he only has enough money to pay 9.6 of them $15.00 an hour, and since people don't divide very well, *he's going to have to lay off more than half his work force! The math doesn't work any other way!* Not only that, but the nine employees who are left are going to have to work more than twice as hard to continue to add the same amount of value to the product, and they were working pretty hard before. So now you have eleven people unemployed and nine others who are working like slaves. Sure, they're making more money now, but they're also paying more for everything they buy. Who have you helped?

A business's balance sheet is called a *balance sheet* for a reason, *because it must balance.* Let it go on unbalanced for long enough and your company goes under. The Laws of Economics are called *laws* for a reason. Just like the Law of Gravity or the Laws of Aerodynamics, they operate the same way everywhere, all the time, whether you want them to or not. There is one important difference between the Laws of Economics and the Laws of Gravity and Aerodynamics though. You can't actually *interfere* with those other laws. Congress could pass a law saying from now on, gravity will pull things *sideways.* It could pass with a unanimous, bipartisan vote, and guess what? **Gravity don't care**! They could pass a law that says airfoils will no longer operate by Bernoulli's Principle and Newton's third Law of Motion, and will now produce lift by magic. Guess what? Airplanes are going to keep on flying the same way they always have. The Laws of Economics on the other hand, are routinely violated and interfered with by politicians who do not have the slightest understanding of them. It doesn't matter how good their intentions are. The Laws of Economics operate all by themselves.... and that is the *only* way they really work. Interfere with them; violate them enough, and you wind up with a country like Greece or Venezuela. If good intentions were all it took, both of those countries would be among the most prosperous on Earth. If feeling satisfied that you (or the person you voted for) have "done something" were all that mattered, this entire planet would be one vast Utopia....

....and *if* a frog had wings, he wouldn't bump his ass when he hops.

Food Care For All

My sister and I have always been at odds on the subject of medical care. She thinks that's because she believes in medical care for all, and I don't. I believe in medical care for all too, but more importantly, I believe in *food* for all, and I think food is actually a much bigger deal than medical care. I mean, look at all the people who don't have health insurance in this country. They can't *all* be sick *just because* they're uninsured. There has to be a considerable number of them who are perfectly healthy. They could conceivably go their entire lives without ever having an immediate pressing need for medical care, but no one, and I mean *no one* can go more than a couple of months without **food!** That's why I think food care is significantly *more* important than medical care. There are millions of people going hungry in this country every day. Starving to death is a horrible, painful, lingering way to go. How can we let this happen in the greatest country on the face of the Earth? It's not only a national disgrace, it could very well be a matter of "national security."

Therefore, since it *is* the Federal Government's job to "take care of us", I think the Federal government should take immediate control of the nation's food supply. I think the politicians and their bureaucrats, not the farmers should decide what crops will be grown, where they will be grown, how much will be grown, and when they will be grown. I think the government should guarantee an *adequate* number of farm laborers and an even distribution of them among the farms and ranches. The politicians will decide where they'll live, under what conditions they will work and how much they'll be paid. Some of them may not be completely happy with it, but I think making sure every American is *adequately* fed is far too important to leave to the whims of the so-called "free market."

Of course the food doesn't do any good if you can't get it to the people, so I think the government should also take immediate control of the nation's railroad and trucking industries. The politicians and their bureaucrats should ensure an *adequate* number of truck drivers and engineers, what they will drive, where they will drive, how long they'll drive, and how much they'll be paid. They should also guarantee an *adequate* supply of the trucks themselves, so they will have to take control of the truck manufacturing industry and the country's fuel production and distribution systems as well. I fully realize that there may be some people who would rather not become truck drivers or engineers, or even farm laborers for that matter, but when it comes down to it, what is *really more important* to our society; an individual's personal desires for a career choice, or the people's collective right to be *adequately* fed?

Of course the distribution doesn't end with the trucks, so the government should also take control of every grocery store in America. The politicians and their bureaucrats, not the store owners (and certainly not the *people* for God's sake) should decide what products the stores carry, that they have *adequate* stocks of each one, and what price they can charge for them, because after all, it doesn't matter what's in the stores if the people can't afford it. While were at it, let's not forget the restaurant industry. The government will also need to guarantee that all restaurants will serve the same food in *adequate* portions, and at prices that everyone can afford.

The more I think about it, the more I'm convinced that even these measures won't guarantee that there will be *adequate* food for all. While some people in this country aren't getting enough to eat, there are far too many others who are obviously getting too much. It's just not right that some people are allowed to get fat, while others starve. It grates on our American sense of fairness and decency. To remedy this problem, the government will have to manage food distribution right down to the household level. The politicians and their bureaucrats will need to determine the appropriate calorie intake and nutritional balance of each individual's diet. Those who aren't being adequately nourished will be given more. Those who have proven themselves to be gluttons will have their excess food redistrib....um....uh....*given* to others. It's the only way that *Nutritional Justice* can be guaranteed. After all, these people are as good as taking food out of the mouths of people who are genuinely in need of it.

Ensuring Nutritional Justice won't be easy, and it won't be cheap, but it will be the American Way. It will require hundreds of thousands of pages of new regulations, an army of millions of bean counters and pencil pushers to administer them, not to mention another army of field agents to actually go into every home in America and insure that they're being enforced, and hundreds of billions of dollars to pay aforementioned armies. How will we pay for it? Easy, We'll just tax the wealthy! It's about time they started paying their fair share anyway. When all is said and done, I have every confidence that our *food supply will be every bit as cheap and abundant as it is in North Korea or Ethiopia,* where government control of the food supplies was established long ago.

Knowing that my sister cares about people every bit as much as I do, I'm sure she, and *you* will be in complete agreement with everything I've said here.

No? You mean you *don't* think everyone deserves to have *adequate* food to eat? You think people should be allowed to starve in America? You don't believe in *justice?*

What makes you think it will be any different with medical care?

The whole idea of Obamacare was to make medical care cheaper and more abundant, right? I'd like you to do a little experiment. Get a pencil and paper right now. Got it? Good. In the next 60 seconds I want you to write down as many things as you can that the *government* has made cheaper and more abundant *without* the program promptly going bankrupt. Ready? Go!

(tick...tock...tick...tock...tick...tock...tick...tock...tick... tock...tick...tock...tick...tock...) (Dee, dee, dee, dee, Dee, dee, deeeee (theme from Final Jeopardy) Dee, dee, dee, dee, deet!... dee, dee, dee, dee, dee....

Would you like another sixty seconds?

Would you like another 60 *days?*

Now I want you to try *this* experiment. Go into a supermarket and see how long it takes you to spot just **one thing** that the Free Market has made cheaper and more abundant. You can scoff at it all you want but every time you enter a grocery store, or a hardware store, or department store or just about any store in America, you are confronted with overwhelming evidence that the free market works every time and everywhere it's allowed to. When you go into that grocery store, keep in mind that the vast majority of people on Earth have never seen that much food in their *entire lives*, much less in one place at one time. Then, come back and tell me "the free market doesn't work."

So what makes you think it will be any different with medical care?

My sister thinks it's outrageous that her son was stuck with an $800 bill for a case of bronchitis. **So do I!** Do you think that was a true free market price for his treatment? It wasn't. We haven't had a free market in medical care for 60 or 70 years, ever since the government decided it was going to take care of us. So let me ask you: What was the initial government action that led to the current state of medical care? Why, wage and price controls, of course!

They were first imposed back in the 1940s as a way to stabilize the economy during World War II. Whether or not they succeeded is the subject of a different discussion. Their relevance here is that once they were in place, companies seeking new workers could not legally offer anyone a higher wage to come work for them, so they had to come up with another way to compete for labor. What they came up with was benefits; health insurance, dental insurance, pensions.

But that's a good thing, right? It gave access to medical care to millions of people who had never had it before! That's a *very* good thing, right? I'll answer that question with some questions. Do you remember hearing your grandparents telling stories about how, back before the 1940s the main driving force in their lives was the need to obtain medical care? Do you remember learning in your history class about all the millions of people who perished every year in this country prior to the 1940s because they had no access to a doctor? Do you remember reading newspaper and encyclopedia articles about how medical care was so expensive before that time that only the wealthy could afford it?

Yeah, neither do I. I wonder why that is?

I can only come up with two explanations: Either someone has gone through every last scrap of every form of media from before the 1940's and erased every mention of the difficulties people had obtaining medical care from our history, as well as erasing that one single aspect of their lives from the *memories* of everyone who old enough to remember that time, *or*, obtaining medical care was not a significant problem for people back then. Which do *you* think is more likely?

You see, if the manifestation of the problem is medical care being too expensive, *health insurance is not the answer, **it's the problem.***

At this point, I'm going to assume that I'm speaking to all the people who *didn't* just throw this book against the wall. I'm now going to explain exactly what I mean, and to do that, I'd like to digress for just a minute.

We all know the cost of living tends to go up over time. The price of everything in general has gone up by about 480% since 1970, so that's our baseline. In comparison, the cost of medical care has gone up somewhere between 700% and 800% depending on which source you go by. Meanwhile the cost of a four-year college degree has gone up **1,120%** since records started being kept in 1978.

Think about this for a minute. How likely does it seem that the cost of the resources big universities have to expend to provide students with a four-year college education as outstripped overall inflation by a factor of more than two? What economic circumstances have hit these institutions *and only these institutions so* hard that they've been forced into this position?

The answer is....**nothing**. To understand this phenomenon, you have to understand how big universities set their tuition rates. The powers-that-be at each university get together and ask one question: *What is the maximum amount of money the students are allowed to borrow in guaranteed student loans from the federal government?* (And if you didn't know, for a few years now, the federal government is the *only* entity from which students are allowed to obtain guaranteed student loans. That restriction is in the Affordable Care Act.) OK then! *That's* what our tuition will be!

You see, the price of a college degree no longer has anything to do with the cost of providing it. It no longer has anything to do with the value of the degree. The price of a college degree is the maximum amount of money the university can get out of the student's insurer. Federally insured student loans are just that; *insured.* They have become in effect, *tuition insurance.* So, when millions of college graduates can't find a job in their field of study, (and that's about half of them right now), and they can't pay off their student loans, the insurer (the government) pays them off. But since the government doesn't have a single penny that it does not first take from you and me, *we* are actually the ones who end up paying off those loans. This represents a *redistribution* of billions of dollars from our pockets to the coffers of very wealthy institutions.

Now I know there are a lot of people who are really into redistribution of wealth (I can think of one in particular.) They all claim to be champions of the proletar....uh....sorry, the *working class,* but the redistribution they favor is *usually* from richer people to poorer people. *This* redistribution is exactly the other way around! So why is there no clamor from those people (and that one in particular) about this massive redistribution of wealth from hard-working middle-class people to wealthy universities. It is a mystery, isn't it? You don't suppose it could have anything to do with the actual product most universities produce in quantities of hundreds of thousands every year, do you? Nahhh, couldn't be *that!*

Now, let's do a thought experiment. Let's say you took away all the student loans, and made everyone pay for college out of their own pocket. Now the cost of a college education is far beyond the financial means of all of but the wealthiest Americans. The universities are now practically empty. University revenues are a tiny fraction of what they were before. With just a few students in each classroom, they cannot afford to pay their professors. They can no longer afford to keep the lights on or the heat going. And worst of all, *they can no longer afford gear for the football team, and electricity for the box seats at the stadium!* In a few words, the universities are going to go out of business.

So let me ask you this: Do you think this would ever happen? Have you ever heard of *any* business entity setting their prices so high that no one can afford them, and then just sitting there and going out of business?

Sooner or later, one of them is going to lower their tuition to the point where enough students can afford it that they can make the revenue they need to pay their bills. *They'll* be back in business. Okay, same question: Are the administrations of all the *other* universities going to just cross their arms and say "Nope, not us! We're holding out for bankruptcy!" That's not going to happen either. They're going to lower their tuition too, and since they are now competing for a much smaller number of students, they're going to lower it to a point *below* that of the first university that caved.

Do you see what's started here? It's a price war. And how do you *win* a price war? You give your customer a better deal than your competitors. Every school that gets into it is going to lower its tuition just a little more than the other guys to compete for those scarce students. Of course, as the price comes down, more and more students will be able to afford it, until a point is reached where the schools have enough students and enough revenue coming in to make a *reasonable* profit. That will be good for the students, *and good for the universities.* It will be the point at which the *most* good is being done for the *most* people. Hopefully the final price will be somewhere close to the true cost of providing the education plus, again hopefully, a reasonable profit. (I know the term "reasonable profit' is pretty controversial these days. In fact, the word "profit" can be pretty controversial. Personally, I was brought up to believe that 10% is a reasonable profit, but that's just me.)

Will there still be young people deserving of a college education who can't afford it? Of course there will, but they will be far fewer in number, and we can help them with privately funded scholarships and grants, just as we do right now. Those billions of dollars which are now redistributed to the universities would stay in the pockets of the people who earned them and be put back into the economy. It would be far less costly to the whole country than the current tuition insurance arrangement, and what is really the better situation: huge numbers of people who will never be able to afford college, or a very small number? *If you genuinely care* about providing education to the greatest number of people, which is *really* the better situation?

How do I know this will happen? Because that's how competition works, every single time. This is not rocket science. It's what any high school student or college freshman learns in Economics 101. Can you ignore the laws of economics? Sure, you can disregard them to your heart's content. Just ask the Greeks how that worked for them. On the other hand, what this kind of insurance actually ends up doing is *disconnecting the value of any product or service from the price,* and that produces the same results every time too. Here's another example:

If you drive a car, you are required to have car insurance. It pays for serious damage to your car, but it *doesn't* pay for oil changes, car washes or gasoline. But what if it did? What if you went to the gas station, filled your tank, paid your co-pay of one dollar, and your gas insurance paid the rest. If that were the case, would you care what the true price of that gas was? You probably wouldn't even *know* what the real price was, and if you don't know or care, *do you think the price is going to go **down**?* Think about it for a minute.

What's actually going to happen to that price is, it's going to go up, and it's going to *keep* going up until it reaches the maximum amount the gas station can get out of your gas insurance company, and it's going to *stay* at that maximum price, **forever.** Not all of that increase will be pure profit of course. Included in there will be all the administrative costs to pay all the pencil pushers and bean counters who process all the paperwork for the thousands of customers who use their gas insurance at every gas station. It's starting to sound a lot more complicated than just paying for that tank of gas, Huh?

So there's the problem. It's not hard to understand, but it's so big and so entrenched that there's absolutely nothing that can be done about it, right?

Wrong.

Here are two things that *could* be done about it *right now.*

How many health insurance companies are there in this country? Hundreds. How many are you *allowed* to buy insurance from, three or four? It was the government that decided that for you, not the Free Market. (Well, the government *with* the influence of insurance company lobbyists, who know that a *lack* of competition means they can get away with higher prices. It's bad for you of course, but hey, it's *good for them!*) What if you took away those restrictions and forced hundreds of health insurance companies to compete with each other for your business? Sooner or later, someone would take the step of lowering their prices to get a jump on the competitors, and that would be that; you'd have another price war.

What if you went to the grocery store, and there was not a single price listed on any of the shelves. You fill up one grocery cart, take it to the checkout stand and they tell that you that your bill is $15,000. You'd pay it, because (1), you have to feed your family and (2), you know that every other store in town is run exactly the same way and (3), you can't afford food insurance. That's what medical care providers are allowed to do in this country, and *health insurance* is the ***only*** reason they can get away with it. What if we required every doctor, surgeon, therapist, hospital and medical care provider in the country to tell you upfront how much they were going to charge you for the services they offer, just like it's done with just about every other product and service in this country? (This is actually not a "what if" by they way. Community Hospital in Grand Junction Colorado does exactly that.) Don't be duped into believing the doctor *doesn't know* how much that operation is going to cost, so he can't tell you what the price is. Doctors and other medical care providers are *businessmen.* They are in the *business* of providing their services, just like a lawyer or a construction contractor, or a computer technician. Do you think any of *those* people could stay in business if they *didn't know* what their expenses were? Doctors know exactly what their expenses are, and if they were required to tell you the actual price of their product, my guess is that you would shop around and go to the least expensive competent doctor you could find, and so would everyone else.

If both of those things were done, pretty soon you'd have *two* all-out price wars; one for medical care, and one for health insurance. Every insurance company and every medical care provider would be forced to ferret out their own fraud, waste and abuse and become as efficient and responsible an administrator of their resources as they could, because their economic survival would depend on it. There would be so much innovation it would be hard to keep track of it.

And what would be the end result of all this Free Market voodoo? After a relatively short time, medical care would be so abundant and inexpensive that people probably wouldn't even need insurance to pay for it, just as you don't need insurance to be able to pay for your food or gasoline. Now, if you *really do* want to put private insurance companies out of business, wouldn't *that* be a better way to do it? True, there might be more doctors driving Hondas instead of Mercedes, but quite frankly, that is the *doctor's* problem, not yours. Yes, he may have $100,000 worth of student loans to pay off, but the return on his investment of that money *is his medical diploma*. Once he has that piece of paper in his hands, he has his payoff. You don't *owe* him a damn thing for his training.

I'll admit right now that everything I've said here is hypothetical. It makes sense, but is there any evidence that it would actually work in the real world? Actually, it already has. Ten years ago having a Lasik procedure done on your eyes would've cost you multiple thousands of dollars. Now, it's a few hundred bucks per eye. It's been the same for just about every other cosmetic surgery procedure there is. Not only that, just compare the experience of walking into any office that provides cosmetic surgery to taking a seat in a crowded waiting room at the emergency department. Cosmetic surgery offices are more like spas, and their customers are treated like royalty. And why is that? One simple reason: *cosmetic surgery is not covered by health insurance!* The price of cosmetic surgery keeps plummeting year after year because the providers have to compete with each other. They are subject to the forces of the Free Market and it has made their product cheaper and more abundant. Those are the facts. I didn't make them up, I'm just bringing them to light.

Would there still be people who are so poor they couldn't afford medical care? Of course there would, but they would be so few in number, that we could help them with privately funded programs. It would be far less costly to the whole country than the current health insurance arrangement, and what is really the better situation: huge numbers of people who will never be able to afford medical care or a very small number who can easily be helped without the necessity of having a gargantuan bloated multi-trillion dollar bureaucracy? If you *genuinely care* about providing medical care for the greatest number of people, which is *really* the better situation?

Now, you may have noticed that throughout this chapter, I've been very careful to use the phrase "medical care" and not "health care." There's a reason for that. If the problem is caring for people's health, *the answer is not doctors.*

Most of our doctors have the initials "M. D." after their name. It stands of course for "Medical Doctor." The word "medical" is the adjective form of the word "medicine." What your doctor gives you is *medical care,* and the *only* thing your Medical Doctor can offer you, is medicine. Medical care is not health care, because medicine is not health. Don't believe me? You will in 30 seconds: Here is a man who takes 4 different medicines for his heart disease, 3 different medicines for his high blood pressure, 3 different medicines for his chronic obstructive pulmonary disease, 2 different medicines for his diabetes, and 1 medicine for his high cholesterol. That's 13 different medicines, so he must be *really* healthy, right?

Wrong. He has heart disease, high blood pressure, chronic obstructive pulmonary disease, diabetes and high cholesterol, and there is not a doctor on the face of the earth who can change that. Doctors can *treat* those conditions, but they can't *change* them by giving you pills. Meanwhile, this man still smokes, still eats fast food every day, snorts a little cocaine once in a while and spends pretty much all of his free time sitting in front of the television. Despite regular and frequent visits to his doctor, he is not receiving any *health care.*

So if what your doctor give you is *no*t health care, what *is?*

Health care is eating good nutritious food in the proper amounts. Health care is getting enough exercise. Health care is getting enough sleep. It's drinking enough water. It's not smoking, not using illicit drugs, and drinking alcohol in moderation. *That,* my friend, is *health* care. No one can give it to you but *you,* and it doesn't have to cost you an extra penny. We actually have *two* crises in this country when it comes to health. One is a medical care crisis, and the other is a health crisis. They are not the same. The sad truth is, your body will only do what you demand of it, and if that is never anything more than sitting on your butt, there **will** come a day when that is *all* you are able to do. I saw this first hand in the Emergency Room for ten years. The even sadder truth is, if you choose that path, there will come a day when you don't have enough of your health left to get the rest of it back. Either you've passed that point, or you haven't. If you have, you can disregard everything I'm saying here, because there is no point in beating a dead horse. (On the other hand, don't short change yourself by letting *someone else* tell you you're already past that point; find out for yourself!)

I'm not saying that what we call health care doesn't need to be reformed. It absolutely does, but solving our health crisis through a massive redistribution of wealth is like solving our illegal drug problem by building art museums. When a government sets out to solve a problem, they should first look at *what **they** did to **cause** the problem*. Undo that first, and see what happens. Yes, the price of medical care is astronomical, but if all you do is simply use the force of government to enable people to pay that astronomical price with other people's money, and then think you've *solved the problem*, you are dead wrong. The problem is still there, staring you in the face, just as big as it ever was; the price is still astronomical! You will not have *solved* the problem until you bring the price of medical care down in line with the price of everything else in our economy. Government is utterly incapable of doing that. There is only one force in the universe that can, and that is the informed, free and self-interested economic choices of millions of empowered consumers.

You might want to sit down for the next thing I'm about to say. The Federal Government has important, legitimate, vital functions. However, most of them involve our relations with other countries, where all fifty states need to speak with one voice. When it comes to the goings-on of every day life *within* this country, there's practically nothing the government can do that the *people* of this country can't do faster, cheaper and better, including feeding people *and* providing them with medical care. All the government needs to do is get out of the way.

Truth and Justice

"You shall know the truth, and the truth shall set you free."

-Jesus Christ

"A lie told often enough becomes the truth."

-Vladimir Lenin

"Just as the smallest unit of life is a cell, the smallest unit of evil, is a lie."

-Tim Retallack

"I won't listen to your [insert name of special interest group here] *lies*!"

He wasn't talking to me, but this time for some reason, I had an overwhelming urge to butt in and ask "Just out of curiosity, why not?"

"Why not *what*? And why are you butting in? I wasn't even talking to you."

"Why not listen to their lies?"

"What do you mean, why not? They're *lies*!"

"Yes you said that already, but can you tell me why a person *shouldn't* listen to a lie? I mean, won't it *still* be a lie *after* they've listened to it? Or does listening to a lie somehow change the truth? Besides, how do you *know* they're lies if you never hear them? Just what are you afraid of?'

"I'm not afraid of anything, and I have no idea what you're talking about. You….you must be…. one of ***them!***"

"Not as far as you know, but indulge me here just a little bit."

Let's say for a moment that you are a peasant in a far away land. The good king who rules the land lives in a castle, which lies at the farthest reach of the realm on a green hill overlooking the moors. You have never been to the castle. It is more of a journey than you, being a mere peasant, have the wherewithal to undertake.

In the court yard of the castle is a mighty oak that has stood there longer than anyone can remember. In fact, the castle was built around it. It has always been known as the Tree of Truth, because it is said that no one standing in the splendor of its presence is capable of telling a lie.

One day, a traveler passing by gives you some terrible news. He has been to the castle, where he learned that intruders from the neighboring kingdom have infiltrated the courtyard and cut down the Tree of Truth not more than a fortnight ago, carrying it off piece by piece in the dark of night. It is the worst crime anyone can recall, and the kingdom is in the throes of great sorrow. The traveler tells you this with a completely solemn countenance (What? Go look it up, and stop interrupting, please) even though he knows it to be completely *untrue.* It is a most vile lie.

Let me ask you this: Does the traveler telling you this lie, and you (having no way to know it was a lie) *listening to it,* cause the tree of truth to cease to exist? Does telling you the tree has been cut down alter the fabric of the universe so that the tree has actually *been* cut down, whereas if he hadn't lied to you, it would still be standing? Of course not. The tree is still there, safe and sound.

Or is it?

You see, there are two possibilities here; either the tree is there, or it isn't. Notice I didn't say two realities, but two possibilities. Either the tree has been cut down, or it has not. Either the traveler has lied to you, or he hasn't. Both possibilities exist no matter how much you like to say that one or the other is impossible. The universe does not depend on your or my acknowledgement or endorsement for its existence, and neither do possibilities.

Remember, you have never been to the farthest reaches of the realm, so how do you *know* if the tree of truth has been cut down, or is still standing?

"That's easy" you say. I already told you that the traveler's tale was a vile lie, and I'm the one telling the story. Well, that brings up two more possibilities; either the traveler has lied to you.... or *I* have.

So how do you *know*?

You're operating on the *assumption* that what I told you is true. No corroboration, no proof, no evidence, no investigation, nothing but my word, and yet for the last couple of minutes, it became your reality. Perhaps that is because you trust me, which brings up two more possibilities; either I'm trustworthy.... or I'm not.

So....how do you *know?*

While we're at it, here are a few more possibilities. It's a possibility that the Tree of Truth has always stood in the courtyard of the castle, but it's also a possibility that there was never a tree there to begin with. It's a possibility that the castle was built around the tree, but it's also a possibility that the castle was never built on the green hill overlooking the moors. You see, the peasants three valleys over from yours have always been told that the castle of the king is actually perched on the edge of the white cliffs overlooking the sea to the west, and the peasants three valleys in the other direction have always been told that the castle is deep in the mountains to the north. As long as you and they have never been to any of these places, all of these possibilities exist. Many possibilities, one reality.

So I want you to give more than just a cursory thought to this question: How will you ever *really* **know the truth** about the Tree of Truth?

You know the answer. There is only *one* answer and it is inescapable. *You* have to journey to the farthest reaches of the realm and find the truth for yourself.

I hope I've demonstrated two things here. The first is that the truth does not need you to defend it. The truth is. Lies cannot change it, even if you listen intently to every last word of them. If someone you loathe, someone you consider to be evil, or even someone who truly *is* evil tells the truth, it is *still the truth*. If the most virtuous person on earth tells a lie, it is *still a lie*. The second thing I hope I've demonstrated is that **the truth will never come looking for you**. It has no reason to. The truth doesn't even know you exist, and if the *truth* will never come looking for you, what does that say about people who do?

It is one thing to go looking for the truth. It can be another thing altogether to recognize it when you find it. It would be nice if everyone were honest and listened with a critical ear, but the fact is there are millions of people out there who think it's perfectly alright to lie to you, as long as they're doing it *for your own good*. In fact, there are millions of people out there to whom truth and lies are tools; nothing less, and *nothing more*. If telling the truth serves their purposes, they will not hesitate to tell the truth, but if a *lie* serves their purposes better, they will put down the truth and pick up a lie as easily as you and I put down a fork and pick up a spoon. They will do so with a completely clear conscience and they will sleep like a baby at night, because they know in their heart of hearts that they are doing it for "the greater good." When these people go unchallenged, very bad things happen. When other people unwittingly pass on the lies they tell, they facilitate those bad things, even if they have no idea they're doing it.

Ask yourself these questions:

First question: What do you think the chances are that the truth, when you find it, will be illogical? Here are a few definitions of the world "logic." (These all come from dictionaries by the way, I'm not making them up):

"Conducted or assessed according to strict principles of validity."

"The science that investigates the principles governing correct or reliable inference."

"The fact of being a sensible or reasonable explanation or idea."

"Sensible, reasonable, valid, correct."

Now this may just be me, but it sure sounds to me like they're talking about truth.

Have you ever had a little kid play the Why Game with you? There are two variants of this game, of course. In one, the child is just trying to annoy you. I'm not talking about that variant. I'm talking about the one in which the kid asks you a sincere question and you give them a sincere answer, but you dumb it down because you don't think they'll understand the complete explanation. Then they ask you "Why?" again, and you give them a little more information, but not too much because you're still not sure they can digest the whole thing. They ask you "Why?" again and again and each time you let go of a few more details.

Here's the interesting thing about this game. Sooner or later, they'll think about your answer for a few seconds and then say "Okay", and just like that, the game is over. Why do you think that happens? It's because you have lead them through a series of logical steps to a conclusion that makes sense to them. Whenever I hear someone say something really inane like "We must learn from the children", I usually say "Mmm....yeah, right, I don't think so. I've actually *been* a child and I know a hell of a lot more now than I did then." In this case however, I think they've really got something. Don't stop asking questions until it makes sense to you. What a concept!

Next question: what do you think the chances are that you will find the truth, and yet not be able to find a shred of *evidence* to back it up? I readily admit that this could happen sometimes, but if it happened with any kind of consistency, then you would have to concede that a large number of the people in our prison system should rightfully be released because they were put there without any evidence. Talk to any prosecutor or judge in our judicial system and see what they think of that idea. Any scientist can explain any theory they might develop to any another scientist, but if you think the other scientist is going to except that theory without *evidence*, think again.

Last question: If you can't explain to another person *why* something is true, how do you know in your own mind that it *is* true? This is perhaps the most useful question I have ever discovered. I sincerely hope it puts a bug in your ear. I hope this question infects your mind. I hope it haunts you. I hope it becomes a permanent part of your thinking every single minute of your life.

I know what you're thinking (Remember, I'm psychotic....uh, I mean psychic!) You're thinking: "I can't explain aerodynamics to anyone, and yet I *know* airplanes fly." That may be true, but any pilot could explain aerodynamics to you in a way that you could easily understand, and then you could explain it to anyone else.

There you have it; my toolbox for separating the wheat from the chaff. It may not be comprehensive, but it works. The fact is, truth is logical, it comes with evidence, it makes sense, and it is explainable, so if you're faced with a circumstance that seems *illogical*, for which you *cannot* produce any evidence, and that you *cannot explain*, chances are overwhelming that ***you're not getting*** *the truth!* That doesn't mean the truth isn't out there; it is. It just means that you haven't found it yet and you need to keep looking.

So, given that the tools for finding the truth exist, they are not kept under lock and key, and they're not illegal or immoral to use, I have to wonder why anyone would stop short of finding the truth? I can think of several possibilities:

1. They're lazy. Hey, some people are. Deal with it.
2. They're afraid they won't like the truth, and they're unwilling to endure that unpleasantness.
3. They've been conditioned to accept a world they cannot understand, cannot predict, and in which they are powerless, by people who have a stake in their feeling vulnerable and in need of protection.
4. They're trying to protect something they *value more* than they value the truth.
5. Any combination of the above.

I have another question for you: Do you believe in Justice? (Hint: the second you put any adjective in front of the word "justice", you are no longer talking about Justice. There are not different types of justice for different situations. Justice, like truth, simply is.)

Seems like a no-brainer. I mean, who doesn't believe in Justice? Well, I'd like you to wait to give me an answer until after we dig a little deeper into what Justice is, and what it is not. Let's say you were accused of a crime. Let's say.... oh what the heck, let's say murder. You didn't do it. Actually, maybe you did. Either way, you're sitting in a courtroom in an orange jumpsuit, manacles around your wrists and ankles, with several other similarly clad people. One by one, you watch the other prisoners stand up before the judge. The conversation goes like this:

Bailiff: "This man stands accused of armed robbery."
Judge: "Guilty! (Bang!) Take him away!"
Bailiff: "This woman stands accused of arson."
Judge: "Works for me. Guilty! (Bang!) Take her away!"

Bailiff: "This young man stands accused of grand theft auto."

Judge: "Good enough! Guilty! (Bang!) Take him away!"

You're almost to the head of the line. How do you feel about what's going on here today? If you say not too good, I say welcome to most of the rest of the world! Ninety percent of all the jury trials in the world take place in United States of America. The reason you don't feel very good is that no one is presenting any evidence. No one is making any arguments. No one is deliberating. There are only accusations and instant verdicts. So now I ask you: is this justice? Here's another question: Would you feel that much better if every un-investigated, un-argued, un-evidenced verdict was "innocent?"

Let's change things up a little. Let's say you *do* get a jury, and you can actually listen in on their deliberations. Their conversation goes something like this:

Juror Number 1: "Well, I just didn't understand a word either attorney said, so I'm going to vote guilty."

Juror Number 2: "This is all like, soooo like, boring!"

Juror Number 3: "I have to say that the evidence against them doesn't make a lick of sense, but since when does anything make sense these days? I vote....well here, let me toss a coin....guilty!"

Juror Number 4: "Hey, this new Android app is really cool!"

Juror Number 5: "Well I just don't have a clue what's going on, but he's just such a nice looking young man, I'm going to vote innocent, Dear."

Juror Number 6: "Are you kidding, old lady? He's butt ugly! I'm going to vote guilty just so I don't have to chance seeing him on the street someday, I mean God!"

Juror Number 7: "I was actually asleep through most of the trial, but what they heck, I'll vote guilty too."

That's seven jurors. Do you really want to count on the other five to save you? So I'll ask you once again: Is this Justice?

I'll take one more stab at this. Is Justice the process in which both sides of the controversy are given every opportunity to present the best evidence they have, are ready and capable of defending the validity of that evidence, are given enough time to make the most cogent arguments they can put together, and after which the evidence and arguments are carefully considered and examined to see if they are logical, if they stand to reason, and if the evidence supports them? Would *that* be Justice?

Now let me ask you one more time: ***Do you believe in justice?***

For those of you who said no, get out of here. You're no longer part of this conversation. For the vast majority of you who said yes, I have to ask you *this* question, and this is the big one: Do you believe that a courtroom is the *only* venue in which Justice has a place? Do you believe that any place *outside* of a court of law, *Injustice* is not only fine and dandy, but that *you* have a personal right to dish it out?

I'm just too cruel. Do you see the corner I've made you paint yourself into? I got you to declare that you believe in justice as I have defined it here. Now, the next time you're presented with a controversy you'll be forced to do one of two things. Your first choice will be to give the other person a fair shake. No matter how much you dislike them, you'll have to listen to them. You'll have to allow them to present their evidence, give it due consideration, and actually be prepared to face the uncomfortable possibility that *you* might be wrong. It'll be painful, even if you end up being right! (There is one possible compensation though; if they *can't* do any of those things, you'll get to watch them squirm!) Your other choice will be to admit to yourself that there are things you value more than the truth and more than justice, and you'll have to admit that you are unwilling to grant other people what you expect from them.

I know what you're thinking; a cute little thought experiment, but what does that have to do with real life? Well, let's say I want to find out about you. I've never met you in person, but I'd really like to find out the truth about what kind of person you are. So let me ask you this: Do you have any enemies? I mean is there anyone you know who really cannot stand the sight of you? Someone who wouldn't cross the street to piss on you if your guts were on fire?

You do? Great! Then I should go ask *them* what kind of person you are and believe everything they say about you, right? You could live with that, couldn't you? I mean, there are many truths, right? And their truth is just as valid as yours, isn't it?

So let me get this straight: if I want to know the truth about *you*, I should come to *you*, and ask *you* what kind of person you are. Hmmmm....interesting concept. If we carry that line of reasoning to its logical conclusion, we have to say that *if you really do value truth* and you really do want to *know* the truth about.... oh, I don't know.... say....

(I am now literally flipping a coin. My wife and son are witnessing the toss. They have been informed that heads is Liberal and tails is Conservative. Here goes....)

....**Liberals,** you're going to have to *talk to a liberal* and actually listen to what they have to say. No, it's actually worse than that. You're going to have to talk to *a lot* of liberals, because any group that has millions of members is going to have a lot of bad apples. You're going to have to talk to *enough* Liberals that you have an adequate sampling of them and can factor out the bad apples so as to arrive at the *truth* about them.

Liberals, You're not off the hook either. If you *really do value truth* and you really do want to *know* the truth about **Conservatives**, you're going to have to *talk to a conservative* and actually listen to what they have to say. No, it's actually worse than that. You're going to have to talk to *a lot* of Conservatives, because any group that has millions of members is going to have a lot of bad apples. You're going to have to talk to *enough* Conservatives that you have an adequate sampling of them and can factor out the bad apples so as to arrive at the *truth* about them....

....and if either of you are unwilling to do this, can you really, truly claim to have any regard for Truth, *or* Justice?

Perhaps the best question might be: Do you pay lip service to truth and justice, or do you believe in them enough to put your money where your mouth is? If you never listen to your opponent's argument, how will you ever really **know** the truth is on your side? And if the truth really *is* on your side, what do you have   to   fear?

Guns

"A well regulated militia being necessary to the security of a free state, the right of the people to keep and bear arms shall not be infringed."

The second amendment to the United States Constitution; twenty-seven words that have been beaten to death. When I first set out on this project, I wondered whether I should even put this chapter in it. The subject seems to have been dealt with so many times before by smarter people than me. But as long as the controversy goes on, there must still be something to say.

I suppose the first question pro-gunners would ask is, why is there so much controversy in the first place? To anyone who is actually studied it, the Second Amendment is clear, simple, easy to understand, and absolutely essential. Let me repeat that first part; *to anyone who is actually studied it.* Appallingly few people have read the constitution, the Declaration of Independence, or any of the other founding documents of this country, and that makes for a dangerous situation. If you don't know the facts and you don't know history, you can be easily misled by the agenda of anyone you perceive as knowing more than you. I urge you, read the Declaration of Independence. Read the Constitution. While you're at it, read Common Sense, The Articles of Confederation, and the Federalist papers. They are after all, the ideas on which your country is founded.

For some people, their antipathy toward the second amendment can be explained by their ignorance of history. The truly frightening people in my opinion however, are the ones who *do* know history and would still like to see the second amendment repealed. I think most arguments for the Second Amendment are inadvertently begun in the middle. Second Amendment supporters try to explain that when you pass laws to disarm people, you only disarm the people who obey laws, and they were never the problem in the first place. They are then left defenseless against the criminals who *don't* obey laws and still have their guns. Maybe this is just me, but I can't find a single logical fallacy in that statement, and yet the controversy just keeps chugging along, so maybe we have to go back farther.

Let me start by asking you this question: if you and I were sitting face-to-face, why should I ***not*** kill you right now? I could do it. If I was really determined, I could reach out faster than you could react, and before you realized what I was doing, I could twist your neck, snap your spinal cord and you would be dead, just like that. The first answer I imagine you giving is that murder is illegal. Okay, but *why is that?* Because it's evil. Okay, but again why is *that?* You could keep giving me several obvious, commonsense reasons, and I could keep saying "Yeah but *why?*" to each one of them until I made you a little nervous about my intentions toward you, but I don't think many people really consider questions like this. People tend not to question the obvious, and they should.

Since there's no way for me to know what your final answer would be, I'll give you mine. I believe that I must not kill you because you have a right to live that came from someplace far above all of us, and therefore I have no right to take it away. I suspect we're in agreement on that point. Our problem is, there are some people who truly don't agree with either one of us.

Now let me ask you: from where does that right come? Have you ever thought about that? People love to proclaim "I have a right to this", or "You have a right to that!", a right to drive (no it's actually a privilege), a right to vote (I've read the Constitution from cover to cover.... it's not in there), and my personal favorite, our implied but never stated, yet seemingly universal, immutable and utterly unenforceable *right to never be offended.* But where do rights originate? Certainly some of them are granted to us by our government. The aforementioned right to never be offended seems to just appeared out of nowhere. But from where does our very right to exist come? It's a good question, because the answer can have profound consequences for all of us.

Around 235 years ago there was a group of men who came up with an answer to that question. They are now known as the Founding Fathers. I want to make a very important point about them here. These men did not fall off the turnip cart on July 3rd, 1776. They were very intelligent, educated men. They had extensive knowledge of the history of the great philosophies of the last two millennia. Before writing the Declaration of Independence and the Constitution they studied and scrutinized virtually every form of government in the world for the last 3000 years. They all had a thorough command of the English language and they understood the meaning of every word they put to paper. They fully realized what a monumental task they had set for themselves. They were attempting to create the first nation of free people in the modern world, and they were creating it not only for themselves, their families and their countrymen, but for all the generations to follow. Here's what a few of them said:

"We hold these truths to be self evident, that all men are created equal, that *they are endowed by their Creator* with certain inalienable rights, that among these are *life*, liberty and the pursuit of happiness."

There is the answer to our question. You are endowed by your creator with an inalienable right to life. God gave you the right to live. Suppose you say to me "I don't believe in God. That's fine, I have no problem with that. You should still be thankful that the founding fathers did. Even if you don't believe in God, even if there *is* no God, God is still a crucially important *legal* concept for this reason: If the people who wield power over your life believe that your rights were given to you by men, then every one of those rights, including you're very right to exist, *can be taken away by men.*

It doesn't take those in power to take away your right to live though, all it takes is one punk with a gun who fancies your car, your wallet, or your athletic shoes. Do you think that can't happen to you? It can and does happen every day. It happened 12,084 times in the United States in 2007. That's how many murders were committed in this country that year. Most of those people didn't think it could happen to them either.

Okay, time for another thought experiment. I want you to imagine a conversation with a murder victim, after-the-fact:

"I can't believe I'm dead!"

"Yeah, but what're ya gonna do."

"No, you don't understand. I had a *right* to live!"

"Well, yeah…but someone killed you. That's just how it goes, I guess."

"No! No! My right to my life was given to me by God!"

"Yeah…bummer, huh? So sorry about your luck. Well, have a nice day!"

I submit to you that unless you have an effective means of enforcing it, *any* right to live is meaningless. So now let me ask, and I want you to really think about this. What makes *more* sense to you:

A: A God-given right to live, which is completely dependent upon the good will of the most evil people on Earth

Or,

B: A God-given right to live that *includes* the right to protect your own life and those of your loved ones with whatever means are necessary to get the job done?

If you truly believe statement A, then anyone who really wants to kill you can go right ahead and do it; morally, there's nothing to stop them, but if the worst ever happens and one day you have a knife at your throat or a gun to your head, I guarantee you that in that moment, you'll agree with me that you are not *required* to let that person murder you, you have society's and God's permission to prevent it if you can.

Sincerely hoping that no one disagrees with *that,* the next question is why *guns?* Because the bad guys have guns, that's why, pure and simple. If all the bad guys had were knives, you would still need a gun to defend yourself against them, hence the expression "Never bring a knife to a gun fight."

If all they had were their fists, then your fists might do, but the simple truth is they *do* have guns, which can kill at a distance, so to effectively defend yourself against them you need a gun too.

If I were to try to cover every argument for and against the right to keep and bear arms, it would be a book itself, and I'm finding it challenging enough to fill up this one, so I'm just going to tackle a few of my favorites.

Favorite argument number one: *"Most gun owners are going to end up getting killed with their own guns."* Let's take a look at the logic it would take to make that statement true. Whether it's in a home, in the glove compartment or under a jacket most weapons are in fact, concealed. Civilians don't normally carry their six shooter strapped to their hip these days (although you would be surprised how many places it's perfectly legal to do so), so you can't tell by just driving down a neighborhood street who is a gun owner and who isn't. The only way to find them would be to knock on their door and ask.

In light of this fact, for *most* gun owners to be killed at all, much less with their own guns, one of two scenarios would have to exist. The first would be that *most* people are attacked by someone intent on killing them. If you can't single out the gun owners, then to kill *most* of them, you'd have to kill *most* of everyone else too. Somehow, I don't think that's happening.

The other scenario would be that the criminals *did* have a way to single out the gun owners, even though their weapons are concealed. Not only would the bad guys have to have a way to remotely sense who had a gun and who didn't, but they would also have to have a predilection for attacking *only* those people who are most capable of defending themselves. Somehow I don't think that's happening either. It is always possible that a criminal, confronted with a potential victim who has a gun but does not know how to use it, could disarm that person and use the gun against him. That is why anyone who's going to keep a gun for self protection is obligated to develop the knowledge, skill, judgment and perhaps most importantly, the *will* to use it properly.

The fact that some people don't live up to that obligation in no way nullifies anyone else's right to defend their lives.

Favorite argument number two: *"Owning a gun opens the possibility that a child could be hurt or killed with it."* This is absolutely right on. We have all heard heart wrenching stories of children who found a parent's loaded gun, and ended up killing either themselves, a friend or sibling with it. Owning a gun entails *serious* responsibility, and in my humble opinion, any gun owner who does not have their loaded guns in a quick access safe with either a combination keypad or a fingerprint identification lock is shirking that responsibility.

With the direct supervision of knowledgeable adults, older children can safely be given firsthand knowledge of what guns can do and how to handle them safely. The best way to avoid improper use of a firearm is to instill the knowledge and the discipline to use it responsibly in *anyone* and *everyone* who has access to it, *but that should **never** include children.* Even if your child has had training and knows to stay away from a loaded gun, they still have friends who may come to visit, and any gun owner who leaves a loaded weapon accessible to any child is taking an unacceptable chance. Parents, if your child is going over to a friend's house to play, talk to the parents in that home. Find out if there are loaded weapons in the house and if so, how they are stored.

Favorite argument number three: *"You don't need a gun for self protection because the police are here to protect you."* This may come as a shock to a lot of you, but if you agree with that statement, you are just plain wrong. If you don't believe me, I suggest you look up a 1981 District of Columbia Court of Appeals case known as **Warren versus District of Columbia**. In this case, a woman was attacked in her apartment by intruders. Two women in the apartment upstairs heard the woman's screams and phoned the police several times. They were assured each time that officers were on the way. After about 30 minutes, when their neighbor's screams stopped, they assumed the police had finally arrived. When they went downstairs to check on her, they found that the police never came but the intruders were still there, and for the next fourteen hours, all three women were held captive and repeatedly beaten and raped by the intruders.

The three women sued the District of Columbia for failing to protect them, but D.C.'s highest court exonerated the district and it's police, saying that it is a ***"fundamental principle of American law that a government and its agents are under no general duty to provide public services, such as police protection, to any individual citizen."*** You read that right. The police have no legally binding duty to protect you. In this country, the police exist as a *general* deterrent to crime, by investigating crimes and apprehending and prosecuting the perpetrators *after the crimes are committed.* If you watch an episode of the original Law and Order television series, you'll hear it said another way: ***"In the criminal justice system, the people are represented by two different but equally important groups; the police, who investigate crimes, and the district attorneys who prosecute the offenders."*** Do you see anything in that statement about protecting people from harm? It's not there. Have you ever wondered why our federal police force is called the Federal Bureau of *Investigation* and not the Federal Bureau of Protecting Individual Citizens From Harm? Now you know. In other words, it's not the job of the police to keep you from getting killed, it's their job to catch your murderer and put him in prison, thereby hopefully discouraging anyone else from repeating his actions. There's just one small problem with that plan…. *you're already dead.*

Police forces in our country's largest cities weren't even established until the period between 1835 in 1845. Before that time, not only were citizens expected to protect themselves and each other, but they were legally required to pursue and attempt to apprehend criminals. Early police forces were only established to augment citizen self-protection. There is a saying popular among self-protection advocates: "When seconds count, the police are only minutes away."

Favorite argument number 4: *"Gun free zones keep people safe, and we need more of them."* Does anyone *really* believe this one anymore? 92% of all mass shootings have taken place in "Gun Free Zones." If statistics showed that 92% of all armed car-jackings occurred in "Streetlight Free Zones" would you insist on *more* streetlight free zones? If statistics showed that most automobile/locomotive collisions took place at "Signal Free Railroad Crossings", would you insist on more signal free railroad crossings? If *you* were planning on murdering as many people as you could, would you choose a location where you could be killed yourself, or a place where you knew *you* would be safe? If the *actual definition* of a "Gun Free Zone" was: "An area thoughtfully set up for potential mass murderers by the local government so that, should they decide to stage a mass shooting in such an area, they may rest assured that there will be no one there to oppose them and they will have all the time they need to rack up a maximum body count", *how would anything be different than it is now?*

Favorite argument number 5: *"The Second Amendment was written in the time of muzzle loading muskets. The Founding Fathers could not have imagined the kind of assault weapons we have today or the destruction they can cause."* The Founding Fathers could not have imagined cell phones. If we could go back in time and hand them an iPhone 6, do you honestly think they would have said, "No thanks, we prefer to wait weeks to hear back from people in other colonies, and months to hear back from England." They could not have imagined cars, or airplanes. If we could give them those things, do you honestly believe they would say: "No thank you, we prefer for our world to move at the speed of a walking horse." They could not have imagined the medical technology or the medicines we have today. If we could give them those, do you think they would say: "We appreciate the gesture, but we actually *like* dying of easily preventable diseases." And as for the damage that modern weapons can cause, it is no worse than an eight-pound cannon ball to the leg, or chest, or head. They were thoroughly familiar with that kind of carnage. They had taken it and dished it out during the American Revolution. If we could go back to Valley Forge during that winter of 1777-1778 and give George Washington and his soldiers AR-15's, do you *really* think they would turn them down? If shown modern assault weapons, the Founding Fathers would have said "Not only do we think these things are *great*, we want one of them in every home in America."

When I started to do some research on this topic, I expected to find confirmation that the Founding Fathers wrote the second amendment to preserve and guarantee your right to protect your life and the lives of your family from harm. To my surprise, I found statements like this:

"We established however some, although not all it's [Self-government's] port principles. The constitutions of most of our states assert, that all power is inherent in the people; that they may exercise it by themselves, in all cases to which they think themselves confident, (as in electing their functionaries executive and legislative, and deciding by a jury of themselves, in all judiciary cases in which any fact is involved) or they may act by representatives, freely and equally chosen; that <u>it is their right and duty to be at all times armed.</u>"

-Thomas Jefferson to John Cartwright, 1824

And this:

"For any standing army to rule, the people must be disarmed; as they are in almost every kingdom in Europe. The supreme power in America cannot enforce unjust laws by the sword; because the whole body of the people are armed, and constitute a force superior to any band of regular troops than can be, on any pretense, raised in the United States. A military force, at the command of Congress, can execute no laws, but such as the people perceive to be just and constitutional; for they will possess the power, and jealousy will instantly inspire the inclination, to resist the execution of a law which appears to them unjust and oppressive."

-Noah Webster, An Examination of the Leading Principles of the Federal Constitution (Philadelphia, 1787)

It didn't take much looking into the subject to determine that the Founding Fathers didn't write the Second Amendment to guarantee your right to protect yourself from a criminal intent on taking your car, but mainly to guarantee your right to protect your country from a tyrant intent on taking your freedom and your way of life. By today's standards, the Founding Fathers were a bunch of dangerous right wing radicals.

To really understand the Second Amendment, you have to understand the circumstances under which it was written. The framers of the Constitution had only twelve years before, fought a bloody war for independence from Great Britain. None of them had forgotten the reasons why they fought it, and 235 years later neither should any of us. Again, *read* the Declaration of Independence. It will tell you exactly why these men chose to defy one of the most powerful empires in history, knowing full well that to do so was treason and would result in their executions if they failed. It will also tell you why, at Valley Forge, in the winter of 1777-1778, when the Continental Army had dwindled to less than 1600 men, barefoot and freezing in the latter part of the little Ice Age, they still didn't give up. If you don't have a copy of the Declaration, here's the relevant excerpt:

The history of the present king of Great Britain is a history of repeated injuries and usurpations having in direct object the establishment of an absolute tyranny over these states. To prove this, let facts be submitted to a candid world.

He has refused his assent to laws, the most wholesome and necessary for the public good.

He has forbidden his governors to pass laws of immediate and pressing importance, unless suspended in their operation until his assent should be obtained; and when so suspended, he has utterly neglected to attend to them.

He has refused to pass other laws for the accommodation of large districts of people, unless those people would relinquish the right of representation in the legislature, a right inestimable to them and formidable to tyrants only.

He has called together legislative bodies in places unusual, uncomfortable, and distant from the depository of their public records, for the sole purpose of fatiguing them into compliance with his measures.

He has dissolved representative houses repeatedly, for opposing with manly firmness his invasions on the rights of the people.

He has refused for a long time, after such dissolutions, to cause others to be elected, whereby the legislative powers, incapable of annihilation, have returned to the people at large for their exercise; the state remaining in the meantime exposed to all the dangers of invasion from without, and convolutions within.

He has endeavoured to prevent the population of the states; for that purpose obstructing the laws for naturalization of foreigners; refusing to pass others to encourage their migration hither, and raising the conditions of new appropriations of lands.

He has obstructed the administration of justice by refusing his assent for laws for establishing judiciary powers.

He has made judges dependent on his will alone for the tenure of their offices, and the amount and payment of their salaries.

He has erected a multitude of new offices, and sent hither swarms of officers to harass our people and eat out their substance.

He has kept among us, in time of peace, standing armies without the consent of our legislatures.

He has affected to render the military independent of and superior to the civil power.

He has combined with others to subject us to a jurisdiction foreign to our Constitution, and unacknowledged by our laws; giving his assent to their acts of pretended legislation:

For quartering large bodies of armed troops among us:

For protecting them, by mock trial from punishment for any murders which they should commit on the inhabitants of the states:

For cutting off our trade with all parts of the world:

For imposing taxes on us without our consent:

For depriving us in many cases, of the benefit of trial by jury:

For transporting us beyond seas to be tried for pretended offenses:

For abolishing the free system of English laws in a neighboring province, establishing therein an arbitrary government, and enlarging its boundaries so as to render it at once an example and fit instrument for introducing the same absolute rule into these colonies:

For taking away our charters, abolishing our most valuable laws and altering fundamentally the forms of our governments:

For suspending our own legislatures, and declaring themselves invested with power to legislate for us in all cases whatsoever.

He has abdicated government here, by declaring us out of his protection and waging war against us.

He has plundered our seas, ravaged are coasts, burnt our towns, and destroyed the lives of our people.

He is at this time transporting large armies of foreign mercenaries to complete the works of death, desolation, and tyranny, already begun with circumstances of cruelty and perfidy scarcely paralleled in the most barbarous ages and totally unworthy of the head of a civilized nation.

He has constrained our fellow citizens taken captive up on the high seas to bear arms against their country, to become the executioners of their friends and brethren, or to fall themselves by their hands.

He has excited domestic insurrections amongst us, and has endeavoured to bring on the inhabitants of our frontiers, the merciless Indian savages who's known rule of warfare, is the undistinguished destruction of all ages, sexes and conditions.

In every stage of these oppressions we have petitioned for redress in the most humble terms: our repeated petitions have been answered only by repeated injury. A prince, whose character is thus marked by every act which may define a tyrant is unfit to be the ruler of a free people.

I have two questions for you: First, does this sound like it was written by men who were hampered by the crude thought patterns and rudimentary language skills of an archaic era? Second, How did King George, one man, accomplish *all* of those things while sitting on a throne 3,000 miles away? You know the answer. He accomplished every one of these repeated injuries by using the British Army. They were the hand of the king in the colonies and they came to be distrusted, despised and hated. The memory of the treatment of the colonists at the hands of the army, under the command of King George the 3rd was still fresh in the minds of the framers of the Constitution, and they were determined that the same thing would not happen in the new nation. They intended to accomplish this by seeing to it that the leadership of this new nation would never have a standing army in peacetime with which to beat the people into submission. So now the question is, how do you prevent a would-be tyrant (or tyrants) the means to subjugate your people, and still defend your country? The answer is, in my opinion, one of the most ingenious concepts the framers of the Constitution came up with: you put the weapons to defend it in the hands of the people.

This is the militia referred to in the Second Amendment, and no it does not mean the National Guard, any more than the term "transportation" today means traveling by horseback, as it did then. The "militia", in the 18th century was defined as "Every able-bodied man between the ages of 16 and 60, and the term "regulated" was then defined as "Well calibrated and functioning as intended." The fact that in those days women and children were not sent in the battle notwithstanding, the militia *was* the people. Every person able to handle a gun was not only allowed, but *expected* to have one. The Second Amendment is not about protecting the right of sportsmen to hunt. It's not even really about self-protection, although that is an added benefit. It is about the right of the people to resist tyranny.

Knowing how much the Framers of the Constitution despised the idea of a standing army, how much they cherished their newly won freedom and how doggedly they intended to preserve it for future generations, take another look at the Second Amendment:

"A well *regulated **militia*** being necessary to the ***security*** of a *free state*, the right of the ***people*** to keep and bear arms shall not be infringed."

Do you think this kind of tyranny can't happen in today's modern world? Think again. It has in fact happened more times in the last century than in all the centuries that came before. It happened at least 12,000,000 times in Germany under Adolf Hitler between 1938 and 1945, (When most people hear the name Hitler, the figure 6,000,000 comes to mind, but that was the number of *Jews* Hitler murdered. He also murdered an additional 6,000,000 Gypsies, Slavs and homosexuals.) It happened at least 3,000,000 times during the Imperial Japanese invasion and occupation of China between 1937 and 1945. It happened at least 23,000,000 times in the Soviet Union under Joseph Stalin between 1932 and 1938. It happened at least 27,000,000 times in China during the Cultural Revolution under Mao Zedong in 1949. It happened at least 3,000,000 times in Cambodia under Pol Pot and the Khmer Rouge between 1975 and 1979. It has happened in Bosnia as recently as the 1990s. It goes on in numerous other countries today.

Grab a calculator and you'll see that we're already up to 65 million people. I use the phrase "at least" because in each of these examples, these are the *low* estimates. The high estimates add up to over 165,000,000, just for the examples I've given. If you add in the conflicts in East Pakistan, Rwanda, Turkey, Iraq and Sudan, the high estimates add up to over 209,000,000 people. That's two thirds of the population of United States murdered.

Now I must ask you another very important question, and you need to consider this one until you come up with an answer. Why are those 209 million people dead, while *you* are still alive? What is the real difference between them and you? Were they 209,000,000 criminals, whose crimes were so heinous that they did not deserve to live? Where they 209,000,000 imbeciles, who were too stupid to step out of the way when guns were pointed at them? Were they 209,000,000 cowards, who to the very last one did not have the courage to protect their wives, their children and themselves? I'm afraid I really must insist that you answer these questions. Do you truly believe that all of the world's criminals, imbeciles, and cowards were spontaneously gathered together in those places at those times to be eliminated from the human gene pool for the betterment of the human race?

It is the very fact that there were so many of them, spread out over so much of the world and over so much of the 20th century that makes each of these scenarios impossible. They were not criminals, or imbeciles, or cowards. They were doctors and lawyers. They were carpenters and bricklayers. They were merchants and farmers. They were scientists and clergyman. They were artists and athletes. They were fathers and mothers and daughters and sons. They were you and me.

So the question remains. What is the real difference between us and those 209,000,000 murdered people? What do we have, and they did not, that fundamentally separates us, the living from the dead? Go ahead, search your heart, search your mind. Take as much time as you need. I'll wait.

All of these examples have two things in common; those in power did not believe that the people had an inalienable right to live granted by an authority higher than themselves, and the people had no way to fight back. It *can* happen, it *has* happened, and in each and every case I presented here, it happened *only after the government had systematically disarmed its citizenry.*

This is not philosophy. This is not ideology. This is historical fact. It has happened again, and again, and again. When George Santayana said "Those who cannot learn from history are doomed to repeat it", he didn't mean your personal history or the history of your country, he meant all of history.

If you think it won't happen here, in the land of the free and the home of the brave, you're probably right…. *probably.* The sad truth is, we are not nearly so free as we once were, and we are not nearly so brave. Whether or not we will ever fall under a regime willing to commit genocide is not the point. The point is, it **cannot** happen here as long as we have an effective means and the will to prevent it.

Here, now, in this country, there are powerful people who sincerely believe that we should not have those means. Our 44th president was one of them. He installed dozens of others at the highest levels of his administration. In 2008, the Supreme Court ruled in the Heller versus D.C. case, that the Second Amendment does indeed guarantee an individual right of the people to keep and bear arms. Barack Obama conceded that the court was correct; that the Constitution does guarantee an individual right to keep and bear arms, but he has also stated openly, in public and in front of video cameras that *he* doesn't think we should have that right. Has the president read all the founding documents of this country? Does he know his history? I really don't know. Evidently that is no longer a prerequisite for public office. If he has and he does, and he *still* doesn't believe that people should be allowed by the government to own guns, then it just goes to show that for some people, ideology trumps everything.

For some people, their political ideology is every bit as commanding as other people's devout religious faith. You could explain to a Jewish businessman that he is actually holding his business back by not working on Saturday; that not doing business on that day actually works to his detriment. He will admit that this is so, but his faith commands that he observe his Sabbath regardless of any hardship it may impose on him. You could explain to a Christian Scientist that if she is seriously ill or injured, she could die without medical care, and yet she will tell you that is the price she's willing to pay for her beliefs.

Similarly you can explain to anti-gun ideologues that banning guns at best leaves all abiding citizens at the mercy of criminals, and at worst can lead to genocide, but no matter how logical that is; no matter how true it may be, it is contrary to their ideological agenda and therefore the facts are irrelevant. The ideology *must* come first. In their minds, if ideology is at odds with history, then it is *history* that must be changed. **Your** victimization at the hands of criminals and the loss of your freedom are the price *they* are willing to pay for the advancement of that ideology.

You are probably not going to be in a car accident tomorrow. Are you going to cancel your car insurance? You're probably not going to be seriously injured or become seriously ill tomorrow either. Are you going to cancel your health insurance? Here's a better question: are you going to let someone else cancel it for you in the dark of night? The Second Amendment is Freedom Insurance. That is not a play on words. It is exactly what the Second Amendment was and is intended to be, and I have to wonder about the motivation of people who so fervently want our freedom insurance canceled.

For those who want to confiscate guns say they want to do so out of concern for our safety, but here are the facts. Every state that has passed right to carry laws has seen an average 28% decrease in murder, a 50% decrease in robbery, and 11% decrease in aggravated assault, and the 24% decrease in overall violent crime. Those aren't just decreases for the people who are carrying the guns, they're decreases for the entire populace. Even those who would never dream of carrying a gun are safer because of those who do. Guns are used to commit violent crimes an average of 450,000 times a year. Guns are used to *prevent* crimes an average of 2,000,000 times a year. In other words, guns are used by citizens to prevent crimes more than *four times* as often as they are used to commit them. In 99% of all those cases, the guns are never even fired. Merely brandishing a weapon was enough to cause the criminal to flee. Forget statistical algorithms; what does simple logic tell you would have happened if those people had been unarmed on those two million occasions?

The state of Hawaii has had a gun licensing and registration program for 50 years, under the pretense of making it easier to solve crimes committed with guns. In that entire time, there has not been a single crime solved through the tracing of the gun to the criminal. Canada has had gun licensing and registration for over 70 years. In that time, it has led to the solving of exactly 2 crimes. In the 34 years of the Washington DC handgun ban, all but one of those years had a higher murder rate then before the ban was put in place. Even in island nations like Jamaica, Ireland and England, where criminals cannot simply cross the state line to obtain guns, when guns are banned, murder rates go up. Whenever citizens are allowed to carry guns, murder rates go down. There are no historical exceptions to these statements. History has shown repeatedly and consistently that disarming a populace does not lead to more safety and security. More often, it has led to people living in fear and dying by the millions.

Again this is not philosophy, and it is not ideology. These are provable facts. Moreover, they are not secret facts. The people who would infringe the right to bear arms know these facts. If they are intelligent men, and if they were truly concerned about your safety, they would not pursue courses of action that have repeatedly been shown to decrease it. They are *not* overly concerned with your safety. They are very concerned with what Thomas Jefferson wrote in the Declaration of Independence:

> **"Whenever any form of Government becomes destructive to these ends, [life liberty and the pursuit of happiness] it is the right of the people to alter or abolish it, and to institute new government, lying it's foundation on such principles and organizing its powers in such form, as to them shall seem most likely to affect their safety and happiness. Prudence, indeed, will dictate that governments long-established should**

not be changed for light and transient causes; and accordingly all experience hath shown that mankind are more disposed to suffer, while evils are sufferable than to right themselves by abolishing the forms to which they are accustomed. But when a long train of abuses and usurpations, pursuing invariably the same object evinces a design to reduce them under absolute despotism, it is their right, it is their *duty*, to throw off such Government, and to provide new guards for their future security."

I strongly believe, and history has shown over the last thousand years that if those with the power to do so ever set out to disarm the American people, it will not be out of concern for your safety and security. It will be because they intend to change your life in ways they know you would never willingly accept; in fact in ways they know you would resist at the risk of your own life. There is only one legitimate reason to fear an armed citizenry; because large numbers of people with guns and the will to use them *cannot be subjugated.*

This was actually the first chapter I wrote for this book. I wrote it several years ago. If it seems one sided, I have to concede it has been up to this point. I still stand by every word I've written here....

....but a lot has happened since then. A very tragic and deeply disturbing pattern has emerged and repeated often enough that it is reasonable to invoke Albert Einstein's "The repetition of the same actions, expecting different results." I'd like to conclude this chapter with two statements and two questions:

First, the statements:

To the Anti-gunners: The Second Amendment is not about hunting, or even about personal self-defense. It was written into our Constitution so that **when** the time comes to fight the next American Revolution, the American people will be able to win it. You may not like it, but that's the way it is.

To the pro-gunners: Even though *guns are not the problem*, it's becoming increasingly clear (even to me) that the *possession* of guns by maladjusted young men from fatherless homes who are continually medicated with psychotropic drugs (and they've pretty much *all* had those things in common) *is* a **big** part of the problem, even though their number is only equal to 0.01% of all the people who possess guns in America.

Now, for the questions:

For the anti-gunners: *If* It were possible to take the guns away from the 0.01% of people who are the problem **and only those people** (and that has yet to be proven possible), how do *you* propose to *absolutely and permanently* **guarantee** the constitutional rights of the 99.99% of gun owners who are **not the problem?**

For the pro-gunners: How crucial will that one hundredth of one percent of maladjusted, fatherless, psychotropically medicated young men *actually be* to winning the next American Revolution? Are you *absolutely certain* you could *not* win it without   them?

Freedom

"Freedom is life without coercion"
-Thomas Jefferson

What is the most common form of punishment in the world? I'll give you a hint. It has been the most common punishment throughout all of human history. It has been handed down by every lawgiver from Kings to Supreme Court justices to parents of unruly toddlers. It has been used justly as retribution for hideous crimes and unjustly to punish political dissenters, but it has *always* been used.

The most fundamental way we punish wrongdoers has always been the same; we confine them. We imprison them. *We take away their freedom.* It is so universally used because it makes people universally unhappy. If it does that across all geographic boundaries, and across all of time, then it stands to reason that freedom is one of the most fundamental and universal of human desires.

I think I live a pretty good life. I live in the United States of America. I've never been in jail or in prison, I have a good job, a home and a wonderful family. I have a tougher time every year making out my Christmas list because I pretty much have all the material possessions I want. When I'm not working or tending to my responsibilities, I can pretty much go wherever I want, do whatever I want, pretty much whenever I please. I have more freedom than 95% of all the people who have ever lived on this planet. I want more. So do you. If you deny that, you're either lying or you lie far outside the mainstream of humanity.

A few months ago, on a bright warm summer morning, my wife and I were having breakfast at a Cracker Barrel restaurant.

My son was it a sleepover at a friend's house. As we were finishing up our meal, I looked out the window at the bright blue, cloud dappled sky and the green countryside of Kentucky, and I was suddenly hit with an almost overwhelming urge. I looked at my wife and said, "I wish we had Logan here, so we could just walk out that door, get in get in that car and just take off down the road."

Why did I feel that urge? I'll tell you why. Because in America, the open road *is* freedom. There are people who build their entire lifestyles around the quest for that kind of freedom. Ask any biker why he rides and to the very last one, they'll give you a one-word answer: *freedom*. Ask any full-time RV-er why they're willing to live in a 26-foot aluminum box, and they'll give you the same answer.

You can't listen to the radio for more than a couple of hours without hearing about some system for making huge piles of money on the Internet. Every one of them talks about how you can become financially independent, walk into your boss's office and say "I quit", work from home, set your own hours, and be your own boss. Why are so many people out there trying to capitalize on this idea? Why are there thousands of scam artists out there trying to *sell* you freedom? Why do people spend billions of dollars every year to buy lottery tickets? Because we all dream of being able to wake up every morning and do anything we want, go anywhere we please, spend all of our time at whatever strikes our fancy. We all dream of being completely free.

How many of us have called in sick to work when there was nothing wrong with us? Why did we do that? We did it because the desire for just a little extra scrap of freedom was, if only for just a few hours, more important to us than our livelihoods. That is how important freedom is. That's how much a part of our nature it is.

Freedom. This is the big one. Freedom is a watershed word. For better or worse, it automatically lands you on one side of the political spectrum or the other. Say it once and you're branded a "right winger." Say it again and you'll get "the big sigh" and rolling eyes for your friends and family. Say it once too often and you're one of those "tea baggers", or even worse "one of those militia types." They are the only ones who spend time worrying about their freedom, right? I mean, we're talking some serious crazies here. We're talking about people who stockpile food and water, weapons and ammunition, who walk the floors at night, wringing their hands, unable to eat or sleep for fear that the government is coming to imprison them. You have to admit, there is plenty of evidence out there. Just listen to the paranoid ramblings of these obviously unbalanced individuals:

"There is danger from all man. The only maxim of a free government ought to be to trust no man living with the power to endanger the public liberty."

-John Adams

"There are more instances of the abridgment of the freedom of the people by the gradual and silent encroachment of those in power, and by violent and sudden usurpation."

-James Madison

"Posterity, you will never know how much it is cost my generation to preserve your freedom. I hope will you will make good use of it."

-John Quincy Adams

"Those who desire to give up freedom in order to gain security will not have, nor do they deserve, either one."

-Thomas Jefferson

"Everything that is really great and inspiring is created by the individual who can labor in freedom."

-Albert Einstein

"The worst way to defend our freedom is to let our leaders start taking away our freedoms! It is exactly during times like these [a national crisis] that we need *more* freedom of speech, a strong and critical press, and the citizenry that is not afraid to stand up and say that the emperor has no clothes."

-Michael Moore

"Of all Tyrannies, a tyranny sincerely exercised for the good if it's victims may be the most oppressive. It may be better to live under robber barons than under omnipotent moral busy bodies. The robber baron's cruelty may sometime sleep, his cupidity may at some point be satiated; but those who torment us for our own good will torment us without end, for they do so with the approval of their own conscience."

-C. S. Lewis

"Freedom is never more than one generation away from extinction. We didn't pass it onto our children in the bloodstream. It must be fought for, protected, and handed on for them to do the same, or one day we will spend our sunset years telling our children and our children's children what it was once like in the United States where men were free."

-Ronald Reagan

None of these men were prisoners. They were all perfectly free at the time they made these statements. What a bunch of loonies! Except for that Moore fellow, of course. He's obviously an enlightened genius.

Here are a few more quotes for you:

"What do you suppose Boone was looking for when he went into the wilderness? Was he looking for new lands? Maybe for something more, something that a man just can't see with his eyes or hold with his hands. Something that some men don't even know they have until after they've lost it. To be free. You know, that's quite a word, freedom. I think that's what he wanted."

-Stanley Ridges as Major Buxton in "Sargent York"

"We cannot defend freedom abroad by deserting it at home."

-David Strathairn as Edward R. Murrow in "Good Night and Good Luck"

"And this I believe: that the free, exploring mind of the individual is the most valuable thing in all the world. And this I would fight for: the freedom of the mind to take any direction which it wishes undirected. And this I must fight against: any idea, religion or government that destroys the individual."

-John Steinbeck, "East of Eden"

"And now we're old and gray Fernando
and since many years I haven't seen a rifle in your hand
Do you hear the drums Fernando
Do you still recall that fateful night we crossed the Rio Grande
I can see it in your eyes, you were so proud to fight for freedom in this land"

-ABBA "Fernando"

"No dictator, no invader can hold an imprisoned population by force of arms forever. There is no greater power in the universe than the need for freedom. Against that power, governments and tyrants and armies cannot stand. The Centarui learned that lesson once. We will teach it to them again. Though it take a thousand years, we will be free."

-Andreas Katsulas as Citizen K'Gar in "Babylon 5"

"Freeeeeeeedoooooooooom"

-Mel Gibson as William Wallace in "Braveheart"

If you care to look for quotes similar to these, you will find thousands, all by people who are not prisoners or slaves; who are perfectly "free." Before you state the bloody obvious, I am perfectly aware that these aren't historical quotes by real people. I include them because freedom is a singularly pervasive theme in movies, television, music, literature, poetry, and art, and has been for hundreds if not thousands of years. Though I've never searched the same media for references to "the Collective Good", I'll wager they are considerably less abundant. You can find them of course, but when you do, I challenge you to answer this question honestly: Are they written by the many, or by the few who wield power over them? People will fight and die for freedom. People will fight and die for *other people's freedom.* People will not generally fight and die for "the Collective Good" unless they have a bigger gun pointed at their back than the one they're carrying.

So perhaps, just perhaps, and this is just a suggestion on my part, we can dispense with the notion that a love of, and a concern for freedom is the sole province of the paranoid and delusional.

Now let me ask you this: Do you think you're *free* because you got out of bed this morning, went to work, to the store and home again, cooked dinner, maybe watched some television and went to bed, and no one arrested you and put you in prison? Is that what makes you *free?* I can guarantee you that the vast majority of people in Burma, or China, or North Korea did the exact same things you did today, and yet the vast majority of those people would give almost anything to trade places with you. Why do you suppose that is?

It's because you have more freedom than they do. Not that you have it and they don't, but that you have more. You see, people in China or Burma or North Korea have freedom. They are perfectly free to do the things that government tells them to do, and they are perfectly free to refrain from doing anything their governments prohibit. If you consider freedom to be no more than the absence of imprisonment, then the vast majority of mankind is and always has been perfectly free.

The fact is that true freedom is also the freedom to pursue your dreams, fulfill your ambitions, determine your own destiny, and live your life in a way that makes you happy. That is the freedom that all of mankind wants, wants desperately, and has not had for most of history. That is the freedom the founders of this country considered to be the birthright of not just Americans, but all mankind.

So now let me ask you: what is the opposite of freedom? I think I've shown that it's not imprisonment, although prison is where it's exercised to the greatest degree. So, what is it? Go on.... go ahead and say it.... I'll give you a hint, it starts with a "G".... come on, you can do this. I have faith in you.... Oh the hell with it; I'll say it for you. *The opposite of freedom is* **government.** There are few laws that say "You can do this" compared to the number of laws that say you cannot. (Incidentally, most of the laws in this country that say "you can"; that actually *give* you freedom, are contained in *one* document! Any guesses as to which it is?) You don't need laws to say "you can", because the freedom to do anything is implied in the absence of a law against it, so *any* law is an infringement, however minuscule it may be, of someone's freedom. I know to ears that have been conditioned by political correctness, that sounds completely off the deep end, but I defy anyone to logically disprove it. The problem is, if none of those minuscule infringements are ever undone, they accumulate, until minuscule is no longer minuscule, it's major.

By now you've already said, if not out loud, then to yourself something like: "What? So you're advocating no government whatsoever?" Don't be ridiculous. In any civilized society, we generally agree that *absolute* freedom is not possible or even desirable. That's called Anarchy and seriously, have you ever *met* an anarchist? They look scary. They're rude. They make children cry. They break things. Let's not go there.

But let's be reasonable here for a moment. You don't have to worry about waking up tomorrow in a country like Russia, China, or North Korea, do you? Your freedom is completely secure, because this is not China or Cuba, this is America and we are Americans. We are a good people, and if our government is of the people, by the people and for the people, then we have an inherently good government. So, if our government gets bigger, then it can only do more good for us, right? Those other countries on the other hand, have inherently evil governments. So the bigger they get, the more evil they will do to their people. Luckily for us, between them and us lies an impenetrable barrier of ideological incompatibility, which keeps us safe from all the bad things that happen to people on the other side. It's been there from the time of our nation's birth, and it will always be there to protect us. It's God's blessing on America.

I have something to tell you about that impenetrable barrier that's given you security and peace of mind your entire life.

It doesn't exist.

It never has existed.

No one's freedom is completely secure, not even yours.

Go back and read the quotes I gave from John Adams, James Madison, Thomas Jefferson and Ronald Reagan. If that impenetrable barrier existed, there would've been no reason for them to make such statements, unless they truly were a bunch of delusional paranoids. You may think they were. You may think you're smarter than all those men put together, and in all honesty I can't prove that you aren't. Only time will tell if history will remember anything *you* say 250 years from now.

It's a hard pill to swallow and I understand if you don't believe it yet. It's like growing up with a big, high, sturdy privacy fence between you and that huge, mean, growling dog in the next yard, and suddenly, there he is, with nothing between you and him except all that grass, and he's much faster on it than you are. This is the reality of the situation though, and you really, really need to know it.

Take any of those evil governments you learned about in school: The Soviet Union, Communist China, Burma, North Korea, or Cuba. Do you really think there is a "Department of Evil", or a "Bureau of Bringing Pain and Misery Into Peoples Lives" designed into any of their government structures? There isn't. The most brutal, repressive totalitarian regimes on the face of the Earth were never *intended* to be evil. They were all simply designed to govern their citizens. They were designed by men who knew with utter, absolute certainty that they knew what was best for their people; that they could run the people's lives better than the people could themselves, and that they alone could achieve and enforce equality and happiness for them.

In this way they are just like us. They have the laws of their country, duly arrived at by their legislative processes, and the penalties for breaking those laws. Every commandant in the Russian gulags, every North Korean border guard, every Stasi agent, were all nothing more *sinister* than government employees upholding the law. If the citizens would simply stop resisting and obey every law and regulation imposed on them, then every one of those countries would be (or would have been) perfectly peaceful places. The problem is, people do resist, and they will continue to resist.

The whole idea behind any penal system is to make the consequences for disobeying the law more unpleasant then those for obeying it, making the choice to obey an easy one. So how bad do laws have to be before people prefer risking death to obeying them, and how on earth do governments get to that place? The answer is simple. They get there by becoming more powerful than the people they govern, either by violent usurpation, or more often, by the gradual and silent encroachment of those in power.

As he was leaving the constitutional convention on it's last day, Benjamin Franklin was asked by one of his fellow citizens: "Well Dr. Franklin, what kind of government do we have, a republic, or a monarchy?" Franklin replied "A republic, *if you can keep it.*" A strange sounding answer, but in what they considered to be their sacred quest to design the most perfect government possible, the founding fathers studied virtually every form of government on the planet for the last 3000 years, and from that study they discovered this:

It is the very nature of government to grow, to expand and to increase its own power.

There is really only one spectrum of government. At one end, the people control the government. At the other, the government controls the people. It is the very nature of government, *any* government, to move from the former end of the spectrum to the latter. Any differences we perceive between governments is only a function of where they sit on the spectrum at the point in history at which we view them, but they *always* move, and *always* in the same direction. Think about it. Can you name a single form of government that, left to its own devices moves *toward* freedom? I submit to you that in all of human history, such a form of government has never existed. The founding fathers knew that the only way to preserve freedom was to bind the government down with big, heavy iron chains and hope for the best. Those big heavy chains are our Constitution.

One of Barack Obama's biggest complaints about the constitution is, as he puts it: "It is basically a charter of negative liberties. It's says what the government can't do to you." He has always been disappointed that the Supreme Court in the 1960s didn't "break free from the constraints placed on them by the Constitution." What Barack Obama considers the Constitution's biggest flaw, is in actuality, the guiding principle of the entire document. The Constitution is not a first draft. It says exactly what it's meant to say, and Barack Obama knows that.

Still you have to ask, how does a government simply getting bigger also make it more detrimental to the people it governs? The answer is, every level of government you add, every new bureaucracy you put in place, every layer of red tape you make people break through, makes the people who make the law more isolated, insulated and disconnected from the people who have to obey it. Dozens of psychological and sociological Studies have shown that the more disconnected you feel from another person; the more above them you place yourself, the easier it is to mistreat them.

If you think there is no evidence of that kind of disconnection here as our government gets bigger and bigger and bigger, then consider this: Under the Patient Protection and Affordable Care act you and I are now not only required to buy health insurance, but health insurance *that meets with the federal government's approval.* That often means much higher minimum coverage, at a much higher cost than many employers can afford. Many of them have simply dropped health insurance for their employees altogether, or forced employees into part time positions in which they cannot make enough money to prosper. Millions of Americans have lost their health insurance. Now let me ask you this? Do you think that will ever happen to *any* member of Congress? Of course not; there is and always will be a separate medical care plan for Congress. They will always get anything they need, whenever they need it, and you will pay for it.

If you or I accumulate too many parking tickets and don't bother to pay them, we can be taken to court, prosecuted and put in jail. Do you think that ever happens to members of Congress, no matter how many parking tickets they stack up? No, it does not. Okay, so you may think parking tickets are trivial. How about drunk driving? Congressmen and senators can drive intoxicated, even causing accidents, with impunity as long as Congress is in session. You or I would be arrested and taken to jail for the same offense.

OSHA, the federal Occupational Safety and Health Administration can shut down a private company for safety violations, but OSHA inspectors are not even allowed in congressional buildings.

Do you think you could completely escape any punishment if your roommate ran a prostitution ring out of your apartment, and you did nothing to stop it, becoming an accessory to it? Of course not, *unless you happen to be a congressman,* who will remain nameless here, but whom you could identify with a little research.

As any government grows bigger, it becomes more and more disconnected from the people. Ours is no different in that respect. Every little bit of power people give up to the government is that much less power they have to keep it in check. There comes a tipping point where the government is more powerful than they are. Past that point, there is nothing that can stop it, short of revolution and violent bloodshed. To insist that something will magically stop the process somewhere short of any Government resembling that of countries like the old Soviet Union or China is like watching a runaway train hurtling toward a small town and saying "Don't worry, those are *good* people in that town, so *something* will stop it."

At this point I know I'm sounding very "anti-government." That isn't true. If you want to talk about the government our Founding Fathers designed for us; that made us the first free people in modern times and the most prosperous people who have ever existed, then I am extremely *pro*-government, but people have been chipping away at *that* government for one hundred years, until most of us have no idea what the original design was. I would also like to go on record right now as saying that I don't think this country is past the tipping point yet, and I'm not advocating revolution; Article V of the Constitution provides a peaceful and orderly process for restoring the proper balance, but by some very objective measures we are very, very close to that tipping point. If you want some examples of this, read on.

A man owns a motel. It has been in his family for three generations. Like those previous generations, he and his family live at the motel. He has been a law abiding, productive citizen his entire life. He has rented rooms at his motel to hundreds of thousands of people over the years. However, an exceedingly small number of those people, far less than a fraction of a percent, were later arrested for crimes, and since they happened to stay at his motel at some time or another, it is declared that his motel is *connected* to the crimes. Under Civil Forfeiture Law, his motel is seized and sold at auction. He is never convicted of, or even accused of a crime, and yet he and his family have been left with nothing and are no longer free to live in their home, or make their living operating the business they have owned free and clear all of their lives…

…. But they're not in prison, so they're still free. And besides, it happened to *them*, not *you*, right?

A man owns a farm in the low country of a coastal state. It has been in his family for several generations. He owns it free and clear. He would like to clear it of some trees so that he can plant more crops. He proceeds to fell one tree, and is slapped with a multi thousand-dollar fine by the Environmental Protection

Agency, because they have declared the stream it grew next to be a "navigable waterway", and therefore it's banks are under federal jurisdiction. This man is no longer free to use his own land in a way that will benefit his family and allow them more prosperity....

.... But he's not in prison, so he's still free. And besides it happened to *him*, not *you*, right?

Another man owns another small farm in a different state. He does not make a large profit from his enterprise. He is barely in the black year after year, but he *is* in the black. He loves his work, he and his family are happy, and he's been a law-abiding productive citizen his entire life. Then, he is accused of and prosecuted for violations of federal business regulations. The federal government tells him that his farm comes under their jurisdiction under the Interstate Commerce Clause of the Constitution. When he proves that his food is grown, harvested, sold, distributed and is consumed holy within the boundaries of his state, never crossing state line, and thus is *not* interstate commerce, he is told: "Well, if *everyone* did that, there would *be* no interstate, commerce, so you're *not* affecting interstate commerce affects interstate commerce and we're going to prosecute you. The cost of the fines, plus the cost of complying with new regulations makes this man's barely profitable farming operation unprofitable. He is forced to sell his farm. He is no longer free to make his living and provide for his family in the way that he loves and has been doing all of his life....

.... But he's not in prison, so he's still free. And besides it happened to *him*, not *you*, right?

Another man owns a ranch. It is been in his family for four generations. He has raised his family there. When he dies, he leaves the ranch to his sons in his will, but they will never get to live there, or raise their families there as they were raised, because the only way they can afford to pay the 50% inheritance tax the Federal Government demands is to sell the ranch. They are no longer free to raise their families in their ancestral home and make their living in the tradition of their family....

112

.... But they're not in prison, so they're still free. And besides it happened to *them*, not *you*, right?

Another man owns a health insurance company. It is not a large company, but he has built it from the ground up over the last forty years and loves his work. He is informed that under the Affordable Care Act, he is now required to except people with pre-existing conditions. His offices are flooded with new customers, most of whom have pre-existing conditions, who put down one premium payment and are now immediately entitled to full benefits to pay for their health care. Forced by the new law to pay out thousands of dollars for every dollar it takes in, the company promptly goes bankrupt. The man who used to own it is now out of work. He is 60 years old and has no other marketable skills. His company is gone; his life's work erased. He is no longer free to make his living running the company he built and to help all the people who used to buy his insurance....

.... But he's not in prison, so he's still free. And besides it happened to *him*, not *you*, right?

Another man owns a General Motors dealership. He started it from scratch twenty years ago, with money he had earned, saved and invested for twenty years before that. The investment he has in the dealership represents his entire life's work, and provides employment and livelihood for twenty-five employees. He treats them like family, and takes pride in the security his employment gives them. He is informed on Wednesday that under the American Recovery and Reinvestment Act, his dealership is closing. He has no choice or say in the matter. Here are the papers, sign here. Your doors close on Friday. This man is no longer free to run the business he spent his life building or to provide the security his employees relied on....

.... But he's not in prison so he's still free. And besides it happened to *him*, not *you*, right?

A woman lives in the house she was raised in from birth. She owns it free and clear, and she has been a law abiding, productive citizen her entire life. She is informed that under

Eminent Domain Law, her house is going to be torn down and a shopping mall built in its place, not because her land was needed for the public good, *but because the mall will produce more tax revenue for the city*. This woman is no longer free to live in her own home....

.... But she's not in prison so she's still free. And besides it happened to *her*, not *you*, right?

A young single mother is asked to make a phone call and deliver a message for her new boyfriend. She doesn't know the person she's delivering the message to, or even understand what the message means, but she makes the call as a favor to him. Though she does not know it, her new boyfriend is a drug dealer, and she has delivered a coded message to one of his contacts. Her only offense was making a phone call, but when her boyfriend is arrested and indicted on federal drug charges, under Federal Conspiracy Law, she is *also* prosecuted, and she is actually handed down a *longer* prison sentence than her boyfriend received....

.... But she's not in prison.... oh wait, *she **is** in prison!* *Still*, it happened to *her*, not *you*, right?

An elderly woman lives in a high crime neighborhood, where she takes care of her granddaughter, whose mother is serving a prison sentence on a conspiracy conviction for making a phone call for her boyfriend. Hearing gunshots outside her window is an almost nightly occurrence and she lives in such constant fear for her granddaughter that she puts her to sleep each night in the bathtub. Though she doesn't really want to, she buys a handgun to protect both their lives should the worst happen.

Late one night, she believes the worst is indeed happening. She is startled by the sound of someone breaking her door down, and she rushes to get her gun. As the door comes crashing in and strangers with automatic weapons rush into her apartment, she attempts to defend herself. She has no way of knowing that the attackers are actually agents of the Drug Enforcement Agency serving a "No-Knock Warrant"....*on the wrong apartment!* The real drug dealer, recently out of prison on parole, is watching TV two doors down the hall. When she opens fire on the agents, they return it....

.... But she's not in prison so.... oh, wait.... she's *DEAD!*

All of these scenarios have been allowed to play out in this country (with you exception of the health insurance scenario, for which it is only a matter of time. That outcome is designed into the Affordable Care Act.) In each case, they played out *under the law, which* means any one of them *could* happen to any one of us. Every freedom *these* people lost, we *all* lost.

So I'll ask you now: Is it *really* okay with you for *all of us* to lose any freedom that [insert your name here] doesn't happen to be using at any given moment?

Our government was designed to protect our freedom, not take it away. Freedom is more than the absence of imprisonment. It is the freedom to pursue our dreams, fulfill our ambitions, determine our own destinies and live our lives in the way that makes us happy. It is life without coercion.

The kind of treatment I've described of a people by their government was never part of the vision our Founding Fathers had for this country. It is not part of the nation they created for us. In fact, it was to end treatment like this that they risked hanging for Treason, and pledged their lives, their fortunes, and their sacred honor, and yet it is come to be. Their successors have betrayed their trust. The safeguards for freedom that the Constitution established have been blatantly disregarded by people who are convinced they know better than we do what's good for us, and we have stood by and watched them do it out of ignorance and apathy.

If anything can be more tragic than a people having their freedom taken from them, it is a people *giving up* their freedom, piece by tiny piece, because they were lead to believe over the course of a century that they are not capable enough to provide for themselves, or that they will never have the resources to overcome adversity, or that someone else's achievements can only be explained by their exploitation, or that they are simply not smart enough to run their own lives.

How much freedom do I want? I want every scrap of freedom the Founding Fathers intended for me to have. I want it for that motel owner and those farmers. I want it for that grandmother and the owner of that insurance company. I want it for that automobile dealer and that single mother, and that rancher's sons.

I want it for you.

I want it for all of us.

I want it back.

I Am an Intolerant Fanatic

I've been told that I'm a fanatic when it comes to my political views. In fact, I've been told that I'm and *intolerant* fanatic. I find that astonishing. By now, it comes as no surprise that most people would call me a Conservative. (Actually, if you absolutely must label me, I'm closer to a libertarian. If I were forced to choose a label for myself, it would be "Individual American", which sounds like it should be hyphenated, but isn't. Go figure.) My views place me vaguely on the Right of the modern political spectrum. What surprises me is that the people who call me an intolerant fanatic are not the people on the Left. I haven't conversed in depth with that many of them, but the few with which I have, I respect and I seem to have their respect as well. No, the people who have branded me an intolerant fanatic are mostly people who consider themselves to be political moderates; who stand in the middle of the spectrum.

One interesting difference between them and me is that they seem content to call me a fanatic and be done with it, without making the slightest effort to understand my views, without even taking a single minute to *listen* to the rationales behind them. I on the other hand, have put a lot of thought into understanding where they're coming from and I feel strangely compelled to reach out to them and try to make them understand me. That's one of the reasons I wrote this book, because I know that people will read things they would never in a million years *listen* to. It's an ongoing process, and who's to say that I'll feel the same way 10 years from now, but this is what I've come up with so far.

The villain with the stovepipe hat and the handlebar mustache, rubbing his hands together and laughing maniacally about all of the *harm* he intends to do to people does not exist. He never has. He is a melodramatic device. In the real world, no one ever does anything that they themselves consider to be immoral or evil. If they *did* consider it to be immoral, they wouldn't do it. In the real world, everyone sees himself or herself as being good. They can't do that unless they can point to someone else who is evil, or at least less good than them. So, people who consider themselves Conservatives, on the Right end of the political spectrum, see evil on the Left end. People on the Left see evil on the Right, and the people who consider themselves moderate see good in the middle and evil at *both* hands, although curiously, invectives like "intolerant", "angry", "bigoted" and "homophobic" seem to be lobbed in my direction a lot more than the other. It is regularly suggested that people like me need to move a little more to the Left. I have never heard a politically moderate person suggest that anyone on the Left needs to move a little more to the Right.

Hard-core moderates (and yes, there is such a thing) seem curiously unwilling to entertain the possibility that someone might be right and someone else might be just plain wrong. In their view, no one is completely right and no one is completely wrong. To carry this line of reasoning to its logical conclusion, you have to say that there really is no right or wrong, there are only differing opinions. That means if I decide to hit you in the head with a baseball bat, I'm not wrong, I just have a different opinion about whether or not you should be hit in the head with a baseball bat than you do. I exaggerate to make a point, but the point stands, and I am unwilling to acquiesce to that kind of a thinking.

Have I painted myself into a corner here? I just admitted that morality is relative, good intentions exist up and down the length of the political spectrum, and that I am unwilling to tolerate it. If everyone is sincere in their belief that they are good, how on Earth can I claim that my position is any more legitimate than anyone else's?

Have you ever heard the saying "The road to hell is paved with good intentions?" The first time I heard it, my reaction was: "What? So I'm not supposed to have good intentions?" That's not what it means. It means that Mao Zedong *thought* he was building a better world. Joseph Stalin thought *he* was building a better world. Adolf Hitler and Pol Pot sincerely believed that they were building a better world for their people, and the people who acted on their behalf were not setting out to do evil, they were simply upholding the law. When I judge people like these (and you bet your ass I *do* judge them) I judge them not by their *intentions*, but by the results they produced, how they produced them and how willing they were to accept those results.

I wrote the following statement several years ago. I took a lot of heat for it from both liberal friends and my own family, but until someone can prove to me with historical evidence and objective facts that it is inaccurate, I stand by it:

Buy some estimates, as many as 170 million people were shot to death, gassed to death, hacked to death, starved to death and otherwise murdered over the course of the 20th century. That's half the population of United States. Imagine half of everyone you know gone, dead, murdered.

Question: How many of those people were killed in Representative Republics, with constitutionally limited governments designed to establish free markets and protect individual freedoms and liberties?

Answer: Zero.

Question: how many of those people were killed in countries that at one point or another decided to march down the road to Socialism?

Answer: 170 million.

More people have been murdered by Socialist governments during "peacetime" than on both sides of every war the United States has ever been involved in.

Wow, talk about your inconvenient truths!

As inconceivable as it may seem to some people, I pride myself on being open-minded. I continue to search for the truth even though I know I may not like it when I find it. I periodically question my own beliefs, requiring myself to justify them again in light of what I've learned since the last time I examined them. So, I'm willing to try being a moderate. I'll do a little bit of it right now.

Let's start with domestic violence. About 1,100 women and 450 men die from domestic violence every year. That's one heck of a lot less than the number of people who die in car accidents, and I don't see anyone clamoring to outlaw cars. I actually have a neighbor who beats his wife. I only hear her screaming about once a month, so it's Okay. Once a month isn't that often. I think it's a *moderate* number.

What? You don't agree? Well, don't you think you're being a bit *fanatic* and *intolerant?*

Let's move on to drugs. I have a 18-year-old son. If he wants to use crystal meth, I'm going to say…. once a week, tops! I think that's a good *moderate* stance. True, crystal meth has killed around two and a half million people, but that's only when it's use gets *out of control*. Don't you agree?

No? Well, aren't you're being a bit *fanatic* and *intolerant?*

So let me get this straight: when it comes to a drug that has killed two and a half million people, or a domestic violence problem that kills a whole lot fewer, I'm supposed to adopt a strict, *zero-tolerance* stance, never budging from it a single inch, ever. But, when it comes to an *ideology* that has killed *170 million* people, **then** I'm supposed to meet them halfway, and I'm supposed to do it while being told that because some people choose to label me a Conservative, *I don't care about people!* Will someone please hand me some duct tape, because my head is about to explode.

I believe in humanity. I believe in the goodness of people, but I know that people are also capable of incredible evil. Some people are baffled as to why goodness sometimes prevails and other times evil. I don't think there's any mystery to it at all. I think the answer is simple, and if you applied it to any chunk of human history you care to, it will stand up to scrutiny:

You will see the best human beings are capable of when they are given power over their own lives. You will see the worst human beings are capable of when they have power over *other people's* lives, and the more power they have, the more they tend to take.

Power corrupts, and absolute power corrupts absolutely. This idea has been demonstrated time and again throughout history, but in my opinion never to a more chilling degree than by a group of researchers led by Professor Philip Zimbardo at Stanford University in 1971, in what has become known as the Stanford Prison Experiment. Some of you may remember learning about it in school. For those who haven't, here's what it was about.

It was originally intended to gain insight into conflict between guards and prisoners in military prisons. Twenty-four male students were chosen from a pool of seventy-five volunteers to adopt the roles of either prisoners or guards. The mock prison was set up in the basement of the Stanford psychology building. Zimbardo took on the role of the superintendent and an undergraduate research assistant the role of the warden. The researchers gave the guards khaki uniforms, wooden batons and mirrored sunglasses to prevent eye contact. Prisoners were given uncomfortable, ill-fitting smocks and stocking caps, as well as a chain around one ankle. Guards were instructed to call prisoners by their assigned numbers, which were sewn on their uniforms, instead of by their names.

Less than two days into the experiment, some of the prisoners revolted, taking off their caps, blockading their cell doors with their beds and refusing to come out or follow the guard's instructions. The guards put down the revolt swiftly and began using "psychological tactics" to control the prisoners. They used repeated and numerous prisoner counts to harass the prisoners, using physical punishment such as protracted exercise for an inaccurate count. They refused to allow some prisoners to urinate or defecate anywhere but in a bucket placed in their cell and would not let the prisoners empty the sanitation buckets. They punished them for insubordination by removing their mattresses, leaving them to sleep on concrete. Some prisoners were forced to be naked as a method of degradation. One prisoner went on a hunger strike to protest the treatment of the others. The guards put him in "solitary confinement" in a dark closet and instructed the other prisoners to repeatedly pound on the door while shouting at him. The guards stated that he would be released from solitary confinement only if the other prisoners gave up their blankets and slept on their bare mattresses, which all but one refused to do.

Just as disturbing as the guard's behavior was the fact that except for a few isolated instances, the prisoners quickly began to accept the abuse with docility and resignation. They quickly stopped standing up for their fellow prisoners, and even began taking part in the harassment of other prisoners in order to obtain special rewards such as better meals from the guards.

The Stanford Prison Experiment was scheduled to last for two weeks. It was aborted after only six days, and even then, not on Dr. Zimbardo's initiation, but at the insistence of a woman named Christina Maslach, a graduate student whom he was dating at the time. Zimbardo himself was so caught up in the experiment that he was content to let the abuses continue. Of more than fifty people who had observed the experiment, Ms. Maslach was the *only* one who questioned its morality.

This sounds like a nightmare, and aberration, an experiment gone horribly wrong, but here is an important point to consider: When setting up the experiment, out of seventy-five respondents, Zimbardo's team selected the twenty four males they considered to be the *most psychologically stable and healthy.* The group was intentionally selected to exclude those with criminal backgrounds, psychological impairments or medical problems. The guards did not begin as sadistic monsters and the prisoners were not people who had already been beaten down. All of them were normal average people, with a desire to contribute to the field of psychology, and were put in a situation where the few were given power over other's lives, and the many had the power over their own lives taken from them.

You may argue that this was an isolated psychological experiment, with no connection to the real world, but it is in fact a microcosm of places like Nazi Germany, the Soviet Union, Cambodia, and North Korea. I defy you to honestly compare what happened in this experiment to those places and those times in history and then come back and tell me there are *no* parallels. The more power people have, the more they tend to take, and power corrupts even those with the noblest of intentions. There comes a tipping point beyond which those who give up power over their own destinies don't have enough left to get it back. Is it really so difficult to understand why I am loathe to give those who for the last century have been accumulating more and more political power over all of our lives any more than they already have?

You may also argue that this is not Nazi Germany, the Soviet Union, Cambodia, or North Korea; this is the United States of America. Things like people being herded into concentration camps, political prisoners languishing in prisons, neighbors turning in neighbors and family turning in family to be arrested, people with guns breaking down doors in the middle of the night and the government carrying the wholesale slaughter of its citizens *after* systematically disarming them, *simply can't happen here.*

Every one of those things *already has* happened here.

Under the Sedition act of 1918, "Speech or expression of opinion that cast the government or the war effort in a bad light" became a crime. People were arrested and imprisoned for the offense of speaking their minds. If that happened in any other country, we would not hesitate for a second to call those people political prisoners. Many of them were not released by then President Woodrow Wilson until long after the war was over. Although we did not attempt to exterminate them, loyal Japanese-American citizens were rounded up and put into concentration camps during World War II, not because of anything they had done, but because of *who they were.* As for people turning in their friends, neighbors and family to be arrested, go to Google and type

"American Protective League" and read the first few posts that come up. As for people with guns breaking down doors in the middle of the night, you need look no farther than the Drug Enforcement Agency, and the government carrying the wholesale slaughter of its citizens *after* systematically disarming them, again, go to Google and enter the words "Wounded Knee."

There is another famous psychological experiment, often cited in conjunction with the Stanford prison experiment that bears mentioning here. It is known as The Milgram Experiment, after Dr. Stanley Milgram, and it was conducted at Yale University in 1963. Here's a brief description of how the experiment worked. Volunteers were led into a room with an experimenter who would act as a monitor, and a desk with a microphone and a bank of switches. They were told that they were taking part in an experiment "to test the effectiveness of negative reinforcement on learning", and that they would play the role of a "teacher." On the other side of the wall to one side of the teacher's desk was the subject of the experiment, who also had a microphone and was hooked up to a pair of electrodes connected to an electrical generator, and to the bank of switches in front of the teacher. The subject played the role of the learner. The teacher would ask a series of questions involving word pairs and give four possible answers. If the subject got the answer right, they were informed the teacher would move onto the next question. However, the first time they got the question wrong, the volunteer would flip the first of the bank of switches. This would send a weak electrical shock through the electrodes attached to the subject. Thereafter, for each wrong answer, the electric shock would be increased by 15 volts, up to a maximum of 300 volts. As the voltage increased, the teacher would hear the learner's reaction to the shocks, starting with mild grunts, and progressing to groans, and later screams and finally, silence. If the teacher expressed any desire to stop, the experimenter would urge them to go on with firmer insistence each time.

Sounds pretty barbaric, doesn't it? You almost wonder how such cruelty would ever be sanctioned by a university. Well, it wasn't, because this was not actually an experiment in the effect of negative reinforcement on learning. It was an experiment in obedience to authority. There were no electric shocks, and the "teachers" were not facilitators in the experiment, *they* were the *subjects*.

I saw the film about the Milgram Experiment when I was in the sixth grade, and it is still one of the most vivid learning experiences of my entire education. My classmates and I watched the teachers delivering stronger and stronger electric shocks, some of them showing signs of severe stress, and even laughing hysterically as they were spurred on by the experimenter. I am sure every one of my classmates was wondering the same thing I was: "How far would *I* have gone?"

The biggest reason the film sticks in my mind all these years later is not the horror of the experiment itself, but the last scene, which showed the volunteer teachers being interviewed before being selected. There was one bearded young man who listened to a description of what he would be expected to do. Unlike any of the dozens of volunteers who came before him, when he learned that he would be expected to inflict pain on other people, he simply said "no", and walked out. He was described by the narrator the film as "having achieved the highest level of moral development." I don't know about anyone else in that classroom, but as soon as that young man said "no", and what he did actually sank in, I was filled with shame and embarrassment; shame to have to ask myself the question "Why wouldn't I have been that young man?", and embarrassment to realize that if I were one of the other volunteers, it would not have occurred to me to refuse.

So why am I telling you this whole story about The Milgram Experiment? Because, by the Standards by which I am judged by a lot of people in my life, that bearded young man, who refused to compromise his principles by participating in what he saw as harming his fellow human beings, *was an intolerant fanatic.*

It has been suggested to me of late that a more reasonable stance is: **This is where I stand**....but I'll stand someplace else if you want me to. Still, **these are my principles**.... but I'll have different ones if you want me to. But have no doubt, **these are the beliefs by**

which I live my life…. but I'll live it by different ones if you want. Does this describe a person for whom you would have genuine admiration and trust? Would you really want a person like this having your back in hard times; a person who is willing to cave on every principle they have? I'm told that to refuse to compromise my principles is fanatical. I say, if you *are* willing to compromise your principles, *you don't have any*.

I am not delusional. I don't believe that this country is hurtling irrevocably toward Socialism so fast that next week, we'll all be living in the Soviet Union, but if you care to study history, you would have to be delusional to deny that we have been creeping slowly toward it for a century now. If you must call me an intolerant fanatic when it comes to politics, I guess you're right. I believe in right and wrong. I believe there is good and evil in the world. I define good as that which produces freedom, prosperity, peace and happiness. I define evil as that which produces poverty, pain, misery and death. I've studied history enough to recognize places and times in which each has prevailed, and why. I stand on the side of good. I will not support anything that moves even a single step in the direction of evil, no matter how far off in the distance the evil seems to be, when the *opposite* direction is a time tested, proven path to freedom, prosperity, peace and happiness. I won't budge an inch, ever. I won't budge because we are no safer in a car creeping toward a cliff at two miles an hour than in one hurtling toward the same cliff at one hundred miles an hour. If stepping on the brakes and refusing to move myself, my family and friends and *you* a single inch closer to that cliff makes me a fanatic, then I'll wear that mantle with pride.

But What's So Bad About Socialism Anyway?

(I'll try to make this the only time I do this, but I'm going to give you a suggestion on how to read this chapter. It's the most satirical one in the whole book. To get the maximum benefit out of it, you must imagine it being read out loud in the voice of a seventeen-year-old girl, and with your tongue loosely in you cheek.)

Why are Conservatives always coming down so hard on Socialism? What's so awful about it anyway?

Absolutely nothing. Socialism is based on a very simple and noble idea; that all people should be equal. Our so-called "Founding Fathers" evidently had a similar idea; that all men are *created* equal, but then they just left it there, like the rest of it is going to happen *all by itself!* Right! But Socialists now, they believe that all men are not only created equal, but that they should forever *remain* equal, no matter what. They believe that our dignity as human beings alone entitles us to share equally in all the world has to offer.

Now, some naysayers will tell you that there's a problem with that idea; that it's never going to happen. They'll try to tell you that some men and women will always rise above others, that this is the nature of human kind and we should thank God for that because those are the people who will cure diseases, who will create new technologies to feed people, to clothe them, to house them, and generally make their lives better. They will be the ones to create great works of literature, architecture, music, philosophy, art, blah, blah, blah, yada, yada, yada. Here's the problem with that: They will also tend to be the ones to make more money than other people and have nicer things, and we just can't have that if were all going to remain equal.

Socialists have a very simple solution to this problem. When one man accumulates more than his neighbor, the *excess* will be taken from him and given to that neighbor in a redistribution of wealth, and that is only fair, because we are *all* human beings and we *all* deserve to have nice things. We can't truly have Economic Justice until every one of us has just as much money to spend as everyone else, right?

Redistribution of wealth is one of those terms that has been bandied about so much for so long that it tends to go in one ear and out the other, but trust me it is a great big, fat, honkin' important concept. The redistribution of wealth is unique to Socialism. It does not appear is the cornerstone of any other political system. When you hear the term used, you're hearing about Socialism. When you hear those words coming out of someone's mouth, you're talking to a Socialist, so it's not like they would ever try to hide who they are by referring to themselves by another name.

Here is the second place people will tell you there's a problem. You see *outside* the ideology of Socialism, there's another term for something of yours being taken from you against your will. They'll try to call it "theft." "How can it possibly be right to take what one man owns without his consent?", they ask. Socialists have an equally simple solution to this problem. They simply agree that there really is no such thing as ownership or private property. It's okay to take it from you because it never belonged to you in the first place. It all belongs to everyone. Isn't that just ingenious? Problem solved! Besides, in this case, it's not one of your fellow citizens taking something of yours, it's the *government*. That makes it all okay!

Some of those naysayers will argue with this too. It's like they've got a problem for every solution! They'll tell you that if you continually confiscate what man produces and give it to another man who did nothing to earn it, the first guy will quit producing any more than he has to, because he knows he's never going to get to keep it. *And*, they'll tell you the second guy won't bother to produce anything at all, because he knows he's going to get it anyway. Nonsense! I've never seen anything like that happen in the real world, have you? If those people who produce more are *really* good people, and they *really* care about their fellow man, then they'll just go on doing it indefinitely, won't they? So there will *always* be more wealth to be redistributed, right? I mean, if they really *are* good people?

You know, even if they aren't, Socialism has a simple, elegant answer. Each person is simply *required* to produce to the best of their ability. In return they are provided with food, clothing, shelter, employment, medical care, everything they really *need*. The products of their labor are redistributed by the government so that *all of us* remain equal and we can *all* live with dignity and pride. Of course, if they don't produce, they're punished, but isn't that fair too, if they won't contribute their *fair share?*

Now, some particularly nefarious people will tell you there was once an identical institution where a large number of people were required to work and produce, and a small number of people took their products of their labor and redistributed it. It was called "Slavery", but there's really no comparison at all. You see, under *slavery* a large number of slaves *were* required to work and produce, and a small number of slave owners *did* dispose of the product of their labors, but in return, the slaves were provided with food, clothing, shelter, employment, medical care, everything they really *needed.* If they refused to comply, they were punished. So you see, they're *completely different!* And don't even *let* them try to compare socialism to prison, because prisoners aren't even *always* required to work, and yet they're *still* provided with food, clothing, shelter, employment, healthcare, everything they really need, so they've got things even better!

Here's another way to look at socialism. Remember this?

"As long as you're living under my roof, you will live by my rules. I will know where you are at all times, who you're with and what you're doing. You will be home when I say, and you'll do what I tell you to do. Why? Because *I'm* providing you with this roof over your head, *I'm* providing you with the food you eat, the clothes you're wearing, the school you go to, and the standard of living you enjoy, *that's* why!"

Remember how **free** you felt back then? How you would walk down the street with a spring in your step, every fiber of your being imbued with an overwhelming sense of self-determination and endless possibilities? Remember how much your life felt like it truly belonged to you, and you were the master of your own destiny back then? Ahhhh......Good times!

Of course, with Socialism, there is one tiny little twist; *you* get to do all the work and provide all the money. But after that, you get to remain always the carefree child, and the government remains always the caring, benevolent parent. They're using your money to pay for that house, that food, those clothes, that school, and all that medical care, and we *all* deserve *all* those things, don't we?

I'm sure you could put yourself in the government's shoes, because when you became a parent, you put restrictions on your children. You had to. That's what a good parent does. How could you take care of them if you didn't know where they were or what they were doing? You were responsible for their safety, security and well being, and the simple, logical truth is, you cannot be held responsible for something unless you have control over it. Responsibility without control is impossible, whether it's at home, in a workplace, or in a government, and wouldn't it just be simpler if they were all the same thing?

So you see, there is not a single thing wrong with Socialism. I mean, who wouldn't want to be safe and secure and be assured of living an *adequate* life? Safety, security, and everything you really *need*....hey, sign me up! That's change I can really believe in. Every single step we take towards it means a better world for all of us. As far as I'm concerned, we can't fundamentally transform this country fast enough, even if we have to chip away at it bit, by bit, by bit!

A Tale of Two Towns

I just love old western movies. I didn't always like them. When I was a kid, everyone in them looked like they hadn't had a bath in two weeks. Their clothes are all dirty and stained and they looked like they were covered in sweat. The first westerns I really enjoyed were Silverado and Pale Rider. I think it might be because they were both set in the winter, when everyone was bundled up against the cold and not so sweaty.

Since then, I've come to appreciate the genre as a whole, and from what I've learned I'm not alone. Westerns are popular all over the world. It's been postulated that they have universal appeal because they are built around timeless principles like honor, courage, defense of private property and the limits of moral vengeance. I think a lot of people like them because it was just a simpler time back then. In our modern world, we are bombarded with more visual images, more sounds and more information in a single day than people back then were in their entire lives. I think that, coupled with all the running around it takes just to keep up with the complicated schedules in our daily lives, we sometimes just like to escape to a simpler world for a couple of hours.

Do you remember scenes like these: A young man runs breathlessly into the barn, where his father is shoeing horses and says:

Son: Pa! Pa! Old man Johnson fell down the well and broke his leg!
Pa: (Not even looking up from his work) Well, I reckon he's gonna die.

Or how about this one: A young man runs breathlessly into the barn, where his father is shoeing horses and says:

Son: Pa! Pa! The wagon train is broke down up in the pass, and a blizzards a'comin!
Pa: (Not even looking up from his work) Well, I reckon they're gonna die.

Good stuff, huh? How about this one: A young man runs breathlessly into the barn, where his father is shoeing horses and says:

Son: Pa! Pa! A cattle stampede went right through the Olafson's cabin! They's hurt awful bad!
Pa: (Not even looking up from his work) Well, I reckon they're gonna....wait, (looking up) are the Olafson's Reepublikins, 'r Dimmycrats?
Son: They's Dimmycrats, Pa.
Pa: (looking back down and resuming his work) Yap, I reckon they're gonna die.

Aren't those great old stories? What, you don't remember them like that? Come to think of it, neither do I. And yet, they must've been that way, because we all know the people are no damn good and won't help each other, right? That's what people keep telling me these days. That's why someone else has to step in and take care of those in need. Otherwise, children would be starving to death on every corner, and old people would be freezing in the gutters, while those who are well off point their fingers out their windows and laugh.

How *do* we explain the disparity between those old movies in the world as it is today? I put some thought into it and I've come up with these possible explanations:

Explanation number one: People didn't care about each other any more back then than they do today, but someone wants you to *think* they did, so they made a bunch of propaganda westerns to fool you into thinking people back then were nicer than they are now.

Explanation number two: Something really *did* change in human nature in the intervening years, and people these days are meaner, colder and less caring toward others.

Explanation number three: People really haven't changed all that much. They're basically just as good now as they were in those old movies, but someone wants you to *think* they aren't so they can justify stepping in and "doing the right thing."

I've tried to come up with evidence, or at least a plausible explanation to support each of these possibilities. For reasons that will be clear later on, I'd like to present my evidence for the third one first.

These days there aren't many significant events that aren't caught on video by someone. You can turn on any television news program, or better yet, get on YouTube and find dozens of videos of disasters like explosions, car accidents, plane crashes, landslides, tsunamis and earthquakes. I'd like you to think back to the last time you saw one of these videos and answer this question: After the disastrous event, what was the *very next thing* you saw? It might not seem obvious until I tell you, but if you're honest, you'll say the next thing you saw was dozens of people who just happened to be at that place at that time; uninvolved bystanders, *running toward* the danger. I'll tell you what you *didn't* see: You didn't see people running up to the injured, asking their political affiliation, and then leaving them lying there if they give the wrong answer.

Contrary to what some people have been trying to convince you of, people have a strong instinct to help each other in times of trouble. They always have. Do you remember the huge outpouring of contributions donated by people all over the country after Hurricane Katrina? It was over $4 billion. It was much the same after Hurricane Sandy. Here's something you probably didn't know: Americans routinely give that much money to charity *every week*. They also volunteer *millions* of hours of their time *every* week. No matter what you been told, the actual evidence shows that Americans are the most generous people in the world.

Now I'd like you to do a thought experiment with me. I can only ask you to be completely honest with the answers you come up with. I'd like you to imagine two towns out in the Old West. Both of them are extremely isolated. The people who live in them are basically on their own. They only have each other to depend on.

Now imagine that a benevolent, but distantly located group of people decide to take care of the people in the Northern town. No one in this group lives in the town, so they must communicate through messengers. If the people in the town run short on food, the group sends wagonloads of food and drops it off in the main street to be distributed from house to house. There really is no longer any need for any of the townspeople to be farmers; it's all supplied for them. The purity of the water in the town well is maintained by the distant benefactors. If the people in town run short of money, the group sends cart loads of money and drops it off at the bank to be distributed. If the town is in need of medical care, the group sends wagonloads of medical supplies. The town has no need for a doctor, because the group sends one of those too, but only when their services are needed. If new houses or public buildings are needed, the benefactors build them, but only when the need becomes great enough to justify it. Should some sort of disaster occur, extra food, water, clothing, emergency shelter and medical supplies will be dispatched from the headquarters of the distant benefactors immediately.

But of course, none of this is completely without consequence. There are some reasonable restrictions. After all, someone else provided the money distributed at the bank, and out of responsibility to those people, there are limits on what the money can be spent on. The care provided by the doctor is being paid for by someone else, and out of responsibility to those people there are limits on the kind of injuries and illnesses considered a good use of that resource. The houses are being built by someone else, not the townspeople, and out of responsibility to those people there are limits on what kind of activities can be engaged in them. It all amounts to good stewardship of resources and that is very reasonable.

The people in this town never have to want for a place to live, food to eat, water to drink, money to spend or enough medical care to keep them alive. The uncertainty of surviving in a harsh and hostile environment like the Old West has been taken out of their lives. They are demonstrably better off than the people in the southern town. Remember them?

They are still basically on their own. No help from distant benefactors for them. They are forever at the mercy of drought, famine, blizzards and floods. They have no choice but to scrape together not only enough food to feed themselves from day to day, but to preserve and put away in the good times to get themselves through the bad. There may be times when the labor, brains and character of every able-bodied person in the town may be needed, so every citizen must be considered a resource and an asset, ready to be drawn on at any time, and as such, must be protected. Even if they accomplish all of this, there are still no guarantees. Death could be waiting for any one of them at any time. It's a pretty uncertain and insecure way to live.

The people of the Northern town; the *lucky* town, don't have to live with that kind of uncertainty and insecurity. Every citizen knows that he will be provided for. More importantly, he knows that his *neighbor* will be provided for. He knows that his neighbor will never want for food, water, shelter, money or medical care. The burden of looking out for his fellow man has been lifted from him. All he has to worry about is getting what's coming to *him.* He can rest easy.

Now, I'd like you to look forward seventy years in time. Three generations of people in the northern town; the *lucky* town, have lived their entire lives under the benevolent care of their distant benefactors. Three generations of children have grown up knowing not only that they will be provided for, but that their neighbors and friends are also provided for. They don't have to worry about their personal security, or the security of their fellow man. Of course, they aren't really any *better off* than they were 70 years ago, but at least they're better off than the people in the Southern town. Those poor people have had to live with all the uncertainty and insecurity of being on their own through all those long hard years.

Now, after 70 years of people in both towns living like this, what do you think the answers to the following questions would be:

- Which town is going to have elderly people who are checked on by their neighbors to make sure they're doing okay?

- Which town will have children who are looked out for and doted over, not only by their own parents, but by neighbors, friends and fellow townspeople?

- Which town will have citizens who are more resourceful and more capable of meeting adversity head on and overcoming it?

- Which town will have citizens who feel a greater sense of community and connection to each other, and care about each other more?

- Which town will have more freedom?

- If some great and widespread catastrophe were to happen, and the connection to those distant benefactors was cut off for an extended period of time, which town would *you* rather be stuck in?

- And now the biggest, most important question of all: Which town will have citizens *willing to give up some of what they have for their fellow human being* because after years of conserving, preserving and putting away in anticipation of hard times, **they have more than they need?**

I believe in the third possible explanation I give for the disparity we see between the world of today, and the world as it was portrayed in those old western movies, but perhaps people *have* changed. Perhaps they *are* less caring; less generous toward their neighbors. But is it because they just somehow changed over the intervening years, somehow just became cold and mean, or could it be because they simply don't *need* to care; because they've never had to exercise their generosity and it has atrophied over the course of the decades? If *that* is the case, is the answer more of what produced that atrophy?

I know there are plenty of people out there who will dismiss everything I've just suggested here out of hand. They will go on believing that people are just no damn good, (well, with the exception of *themselves* and the people they vote for, of course.) To them I'll just say this one last thing. They seem content to think that it "just somehow happened." My explanation offers a cause and effect relationship. Some scientists say that there may be other universes out there that are so different from ours that effects may proceed causes at random, but we still live in this one, where a cause preceding an effect makes a whole lot more sense, and speaking strictly for myself, gives me a lot more hope for the future.

Global Warming
(Uh, sorry…. *Climate Change*)

The debate is over. The science is settled. Anthropogenic global warming is destroying the Earth. The polar ice caps will melt, the seas will rise, and deserts will swallow the continents. Mankind and most of the animal kingdom will perish. We must take drastic action now to reduce the emission of greenhouse gases if we are to save our planet from global disaster. That's what the scientists are saying.

I would be a lot more quiescent about what the scientists are *saying* if what they're *doing* was science. It isn't.

In the first place, in science, the debate is never over…. as in **never.** Science is always open to new evidence. If it wasn't, the earth would still be flat, the sun would revolve around it, you could turn lead into gold, you could treat most diseases by bleeding people, and so on. *Real* science is never, ever settled.

Secondly, the scientific method is not just a catchphrase for anything and everything scientists may feel like doing. The scientific method is a standardized process, involving the same steps, applied in the same order every time. For those of you who aren't familiar with the steps of the scientific method, here they are:

1. Make an observation.
2. Ask a question.
3. Gather known information to formulate a hypothesis.
4. Design an experiment to test your hypothesis.
5. Carry out the experiment and record your findings
6. Repeat the experiment to confirm your findings.

7. Share your work with others so they can check your work and repeat the experiment themselves.

The whole process is set off by someone making an observation. You observe A and B. You notice that B often follows A in time and you start to wonder if there might be a cause and effect relationship. Some people don't even make it to step 2 of the scientific process. They just assume that since B follows A, then A must have caused B. They're sitting at a railroad crossing waiting for a train to pass, they sneeze, and 10 seconds later, the train derails. They conclude that sneezing causes train derailment. Don't laugh; I've met some of these people. They walk among us. Now you see why we need science.

The reason we have to ask the question is because A *doesn't* always cause B. I'll give you a good example: The more churches any given city has, the more alcoholics it will have. That's a very common correlation. We can then conclude that religion causes alcoholism, right? Wrong. How do we know that alcoholism doesn't cause religion? In reality, the number of churches in the city and the number of alcoholics it has are both functions of the size of its population. Sometimes A causes B, sometimes B causes A. Sometimes A and B are both caused by anything from C through Z, and they have nothing whatsoever to do with each other. Correlation does not imply causality. If you're a budding scientist, write that down. Learn it, know it, live it. If you're a budding *politician*….aah, never mind, you won't need it.

With global warming, the observation supposedly was this: The earth was getting warmer. (Notice I use the word "was" and I'll get to that more later on.) Now that we have our observation, we need to ask our question, which in this case is, *why* was the earth getting warmer? Next, we take a look around and gather information to form a hypothesis. We notice that the planet Venus, which has an atmosphere composed almost entirely of carbon dioxide is extremely warm, as in "lead melting at your feet" warm. We also know that the burning of fossil fuels produces carbon, which is a component of carbon dioxide, as a byproduct. We can now formulate a hypothesis, which is: The burning of fossil fuels is putting carbon dioxide into our atmosphere, which is causing a greenhouse effect similar to Venus's and warming the Earth.

So far so good, we're using the scientific method, right? Technically yes; we've got a touch of tunnel vision, but we'll work with it. It's time to design an experiment. We have a standard template for this. It's called the Double Blind Control Experiment. Here's how it works. We want to determine if *Cause A* produces *Effect B*. We divide our test subjects into three groups; Group 1, Group 2 and the Control Group. We need to isolate these groups as much as we can from any outside influences because we want to make sure that one *and only one* factor is observed to be acting on the subjects. We single out *Cause A* and expose Group 1 to it. At the same time, we expose Group 2 to a *placebo*; something which appears just like *Cause A*, but that we know has no effect. This is to prevent Group 1 from imagining that they are being affected by something that they alone are exposed to. If *Cause A* truly does produce *Effect B*, and we should observe *Effect B* appearing in Group 1 and *not* in Group 2. To the Control Group, we do nothing. This is to make sure that *Effect B* isn't caused by causes C through Z. If we see *Effect B* show up in the Control Group, we know that *Cause A* has nothing to do with *Effect B*, and we have to start over from scratch and design a new and different experiment.

The reason we call this a *double blind experiment* is that neither the test subjects nor the people conducting the experiment know which group is being exposed to *Cause A* and which is getting the placebo until after the experiment is over. That way, none of them have a chance to unconsciously influence the outcome of the experiment through their behaviors, attitudes, or biases.

Pretty cool process, huh? It's not even half over. Now we run the experiment the other way, with Group 1 getting the placebo and Group 2 getting *Cause A*. You've probably already guessed why. If *Cause A* really does produce *Effect B*, then we should now see it showing up in Group 2 and not in Group 1 or the Control Group. If we see that, then you might think the experiment has been a success, but experiments neither succeed nor fail, they simply produce results.

The next step in the process is to run the whole thing over again a second time with a different Group 1, a different Group 2 and a different Control Group to see if you can reproduce the results of the first round of the experiment. This is a very important step in the process, because any result that is *not reproducible* has no scientific value.

Given that the experiment has been run carefully following the steps of the scientific process, there is very little chance that anyone has screwed up, but we're going to reduce that chance even more by submitting the results of our experiment to *Peer Review*. We publish everything about our experiment, including every detail about how we conducted it, so that every other scientist in our field can comb through it and pick it over, looking for anything we did wrong or any inconsistencies in our findings.

Believe it or not, the process isn't even over yet. At this point, someone else steps up and repeats the experiment all over again, from beginning to end. If, after several repetitions by different teams of experimenters, the results are still consistent, then and *only* then do we declare that *the evidence supports the hypothesis.*

So there you have it, an overview of the Scientific Method. It is consistent; it is eternal. Now let's take a look at how we would use the Scientific Method to prove Global Warming. You can skim through this part if you've already deduced where I'm going, but you might get a yuk out of it anyway.

First, you gather together your Earth 1, Earth 2 and your Control Earth. You somehow find a way to isolate all three Earths from the Sun, the Solar System, and the rest of the Universe. Then you burn fossil fuels on Earth 1 for a few hundred years, while burning some sort of placebo fuel on Earth 2 that simulates fossil fuels in every observable away but does not produce any carbon.

To the Control Earth, you do nothing. After those few hundred years, you see if Earth 1 has experienced any warming and that both Earth 2 and the Control Earth have not. Then you switch planets and burn fossil fuels on Earth 2 while Earth 1 gets the placebo fuel. You record all of your findings and repeat the experiment again with your next three Earths. Then you publish all of your results, let your peers review it, and wait for some of them to repeat the experiment again with another three…. excuse me, another *six* Earths.

It is impossible to use the Scientific Method to prove Global Warming. So how *did* the scientists come to the conclusion that the Earth is doomed unless we stop the burning oil, coal and natural gas right freakin' now?

The answer is computer models. They programmed everything they know about Earth's climate and the way it reacts to the addition of greenhouse gases into their computers. They build a virtual Earth inside the computer, they plug in the values of how fast we're adding carbon dioxide and then fast forward the computer a few hundred years to see what the program predicts.

Notice I said they program a computer with *everything they know* about the Earth's climate and how it behaves? If they knew *everything* about the Earth's climate, there would be no need for any more climate or weather research and no one would ever again die or be injured in a weather related event. Our climate and weather are almost inconceivably complex. Chaos Theory and the Butterfly Effect come into play here more than in almost any other area of science. Any meteorologist will tell you that weather forecasts are notoriously inaccurate any more than 24 hours into the future, and meteorologists are the only people on Earth to go to school for six years, get a 40% on every test, and pass with an A. There is still plenty they don't know, and therefore they cannot build a *completely accurate* computer model.

You can plug the *same* values into the *same* computer model ten different times and get ten different results. Here's the real kicker: When they put the *known* values from the past into the computer models they've used to produce their global warming conclusions, those very computer models *cannot accurately predict the present*. If they can't predict the present, why would anyone conclude that they can predict the future? So the question remains: if scientists haven't used computer models or the Scientific Method to prove Global Warming, how *did* they prove it?

They *didn't* prove it. They *can't* prove it. Even if they did have twelve Earths, someplace to isolate them from the Universe, a magic placebo fuel, and twelve hundred years to run the experiment, they still couldn't *prove* anything. I'm going to let you in on a little secret. (This is where I beckon you closer with my finger and you lean over and put your ear to my mouth for me to whisper into it) Are you ready? Here it is:

In all of human history, science has never *proven* anything. Within the Scientific Method, the evidence can either support a hypothesis or.... *fail to support it!* That's it. That's all it can do, and any true scientist will be the first one to tell you that.

Still, we *have* to believe in global warming. It's what all the scientists are *saying*, isn't it? That course of action would be based on two assumptions. The first is that all of the scientists are on the global warming bandwagon. They aren't. Do you have any idea how many scientists there are in the world? Do you know what fraction of them have jumped on the bandwagon? Do you know how many of the scientists *on* the bandwagon are astrophysicists, or volcanologists, or mycologists, or some other kind of scientists who don't know any more about climatology than you or I?

The other assumption is one so basic, I don't think most people even realize they're making it, and that is the *assumption that scientists never lie*. How in hell did we ever conclude that? There is no equivalent of the Hippocratic Oath for scientists. They do not raise their right hands, place their left hands on a copy of the Theory of Relativity the day they get their science license and swear that they will always tell the truth. Can anyone show me concrete evidence that a scientist with an agenda is any less likely to lie to advance it than a politician with an agenda?

But why, you may ask, would a scientist lie about this? What would be their motivation? The same thing that motivates everyone else....money! It takes a lot of money for scientists to run their experiments. I mean honestly, can you imagine how much six planet Earths and a galactic isolation chamber are going to set you back? Speaking out in favor of the global warming hypothesis is a good way to get tons of grant money, and speaking out *against* it is a good way to see your finances dry up, forever. No folks, I know you were hoping for a break from this, and I'm sorry to have to drag you back here again, but Global Warming is not science, it's politics.

So, am I saying that global warming is a hoax? Am I saying that it hasn't happened? No, global warming is very real. 18,000 years ago a large portion of the earth was covered in a couple of miles of ice. Now, it isn't. That necessarily takes quite a bit of warming. When the whole global warming debate started, the Earth *was* getting warmer. 300 years before that, it was getting colder. For nine thousand years before that, it was getting warmer. For millions of years before that, it was yo-yoing wildly back-and-forth between hotter and colder. Before that, it was warmer for a long, long time. Before that, it was a hell of a lot colder. 700 million years ago, the entire planet was frozen up like a big snowball. Its climate has been changing for as long as we can look back. Look at any accurate graph of the Earth's temperature over time, and you will never, *ever* see a straight line. What does that tell you? Climate is *always* changing. *That's* what climate *does*.

You'd think that somewhere along this whole global warming trail, at least *some* scientists would've noticed that. I would like to ask a group of global warming scientists exactly how they conclusively determined that the temperature we're experiencing in the tiny little geological blink of an eye that is the tenure of humans on this planet, to be the only *correct* temperature for the Earth. Some will put forth the argument that "Well it's the temperature at which humans and their agriculture can thrive." Isn't that elevating humans over nature? That sounds pretty anthropocentric to me; not a very environmentalist point of view.

There is no normal or correct temperature for the Earth. Now, if you want to talk about the *average* temperature of the earth over the course of its entire existence, that's actually much warmer than it is today, and yet life has flourished. To claim that a planet's average temperature is going to destroy it is not only unscientific, it's illogical.

Have you noticed that you often hear people talking about how the hottest years on record are all in the last decade? Here's the interesting thing about the phrase "on record." In and of itself, it means nothing. Any year being the hottest, or coldest, or driest, or wettest on record is nothing more than a function of where we are in time now, and when the records started being kept. If the records had been started in the Little Ice Age, then yes, recent years have been the hottest on record. If the records had been started during the Permian Period, Then we would be living in some of the coldest years on record. If the records have been started two years ago, and this winter is colder than the last, then this winter is the coldest on record. But, the records were started when they were, and we are where we are now, and that is the only reason those statements are true.

And actually, they're not even true anymore. Since 1998, weather satellites monitoring the Earth *have detected no increase in its temperature.* That means all the radical, extreme weather that has developed since then; all the alarming increases in tornados, and hurricanes, and tsunamis and every other weather phenomenon that's been urgently brought to your attention every day and week and year over the last two decades, *has developed in a thermally stable atmosphere.* Now, some scientists are saying they have no idea what is causing the current trend, but they are certain that global warming will start back up again in another twenty to thirty years. Think about that and answer me this: If you have no idea what is causing a phenomenon, how can you predict how long it will last? That's like your mechanic saying "I have no idea what's wrong with your car, but it will fix itself on the 24th of next month."

My point in all this is not that global warming does not exist; it absolutely does. My point is that the current panic about global warming that certain entities are attempting to instill in humanity has nothing to do with science and everything to do with ideology. Its object is not to save the Earth, but to drive it toward Socialism. If you'd like evidence of this, let's examine one of the main strategies with which governments have proposed to deal with it. It's called "Cap and Trade." If you're not familiar with how it works, here's the gist: Each of the world's countries is given a carbon allowance, based on the supposed calculated amount of carbon dioxide which can be safely released into the atmosphere, and the supposed calculated amount each country needs. And who will be issuing the carbon credits? Well, since this process involves nearly every country in the world, what organization would be the logical choice? Yes, let's see....where are we going to find an international organization made up of representatives from nearly every country on earth? Where, oh where, oh where? This is truly a tricky one!

Anyhow, if a country uses up all its carbon credits, it can buy extra credits from countries that have not yet used theirs up. Sounds fair, doesn't it? Sounds like it will work? Let me ask you this, and I want you to really think about it. As a matter of fact, this is the *one* question I hope sticks in your mind and bugs you on your afternoon drive home from work every day: If carbon, which is literally the building block of life on earth, and carbon dioxide, *without* which life on Earth literally *would not exist* are such dire threats to all life on earth, why would *anyone* be allotted ***more than they need?***

Here are a couple more good questions: Why only *carbon dioxide?* There are several more potent greenhouse gases, the *most* potent of which is actually water vapor. Not only is it several times more potent, it's up to a hundred times more prevalent in the atmosphere (0.04% for carbon dioxide, and 2-3% for water vapor.) If carbon dioxide has been declared a "dangerous pollutant" by the Environmental Protection Agency because it is a greenhouse gas, and water vapor is a much more potent and prevalent greenhouse gas, then why has water vapor not *also* been declared a dangerous pollutant by the EPA? You don't suppose it could be due to the fact that water vapor is not produced in any great amounts by human economic activity, and therefore you cannot *control* human economic activity by regulating it, do you? Naaaah....couldn't be *that!* Incidentally, water vapor, the most potent greenhouse in existence, is the *only* byproduct of burning hydrogen, and yet environmental activists, scientists and futurists have seriously proposed a "hydrogen economy" as a potential solution to global warming. Curious, very curious.

This next question is a bit of a thought experiment, but I'm going to ask it anyway. If it's too much mental effort for some people to put out, so be it; I'll take my chances. If there were to be invented a simple, inexpensive device that could be attached to the exhaust of any internal combustion engine, that would literally suck up all the carbon coming out of it, leaving nothing but oxygen being put back into the atmosphere, *and* this device *was* installed on every internal combustion engine on Earth, *would the global warming issue simply go away?* Would the United Nations Intergovernmental Panel on Climate Change just *disband?* Would every governmental entity that has invested so much time and effort into solving this international, global, planetary crises simply throw up its hands and say "Well, the problem is solved, the danger is completely over. You can all go back to burning as much fossil fuel as you need to because it's no longer a threat?" Can you *really* see that happening, and if not....why?

I'm going to leave you completely on your own for the answers to those second two, but I'm going to offer an answer to the Cap and Trade question, which is this: It's not the *"Cap"* They're after, it's the *"Trade."* I don't know if you were aware of this, but I am able to predict the future. (You can too, by the way. Anyone can *predict* the future; the trick is having those predictions come true.) This time however, I'm going to predict the future with 100% accuracy:

If Cap and Trade is ever put into place on an international level, undeveloped third world countries will be given far more carbon credits than they will ever need. The United States will be given far fewer than it can possibly make do with. Every American corporation will be forced by international law to buy carbon credits from undeveloped countries *simply to be allowed to exist.* Just as with corporate taxes, they will not sacrifice their existence to pay these credits out of their own profits. The money will be taken out of every American worker's pocket in the form of higher prices for everything they really do need, just as surely as corporate taxes are now. Unlike those taxes, the money they pay will not benefit them in anyway; it will leave the country. The flow will be one way. The wealth that we Americans produce with our entrepreneurial spirit, our innovation, our imaginations, and the sweat of our brows, will leave our nation and be redistributed among the other nations of the world. It will never come back. That's not a bug in the programming. It's not a flaw in the plan. That *is* the plan. That's exactly how it's meant to work. The Earth's temperature may rise and it may fall, but this much is absolutely inevitable. If anyone wants to wager ten million dollars that I'm wrong, I will gladly take the bet. Global Warming is not about saving the Earth. It's about involuntary global centralization of power and redistribution of wealth.

I'd like to end this chapter on a particularly radical note. I hope by now, what I've written has inspired you to read the Declaration of Independence. If you have, good for you…. *and* good for *me!* If you haven't, then I have two challenges for you: First, grab any dictionary and look up the word "trade" and the word "extortion." Then come back and tell me which of these definitions *best* describes Cap and Trade. The second challenge is this: Read the Declaration of Independence. Read the United States Constitution. Then go a step further and read the Communist Manifesto and Das Kapital. Then, come back and tell me in which of these texts you found the phrase "the Redistribution of Wealth."

Overpopulation

"Futurists don't consider overpopulation to be *one* of the issues of the future, they consider it to be *the* issue of the future.

-Dan Brown, Author

"The human population issue is the topic I see has the most vital to solve if our children and grandchildren are to have a good quality of life."

-Alexandra Paul, Actress

"...the chief cause for the impending collapse of the world; the cause sufficient in and of itself is the enormous growth of the human population; the human flood. The worst enemy of life is too much life; the excess of *human* life."

-Pennti Linkola, Ecologist

"Improve your life by taking advantage of new technologies like bleach or a drinking glass. Show your love of the globe by reducing an overpopulated world by one."

-Jarod Kintz, Author

"The ecological crisis, in short, is the population crisis. Cut the population by 90%, and there aren't enough people left to do a great deal of ecological damage.

-Mikhail Gorbachev, former General Secretary, Communist Party of the Soviet Union

"In the event that I am reincarnated, I wish to return as a deadly virus, in order to contribute something to solve overpopulation."

-Prince Phillip, Duke of Edinburgh

"Short of nuclear war itself, population growth is the gravest issue the world faces. If we do not act, the problem will be solved by famine, riots, insurrection and war."

-Robert Macnamara, former World Bank President

Just how overpopulated is the Earth? It must be a pretty serious problem if very smart people are advocating exterminating 90% of the world's population, nuclear war, mass suicide and even cannibalism to solve it. We have to believe them, don't we? How could all of those "futurists" not know what they're talking about?

Well, let me tell you something about "futurists." They're the guys who are constantly telling us that computers will one day become more intelligent than humans, and they will rise up, take over the Earth and we will be their slaves. You know what I say to that? *Not unless you give them arms and legs and no OFF switch!* I really just have one thing to say to "futurists." **Where's my flying car?** You told me I was going to have a flying car like....*twenty years ago!* Well....*where is it? **I want my flying car!***

Seriously though, some of them are very smart, I guess. Stephen Hawking, one of the smartest people in the world said: "In the last 200 years the population of our planet has grown exponentially at a rate of 1.9% per year. If it continues at this rate, with population doubling every 40 years, by 2600 we will all be standing literally shoulder-to-shoulder." A very scary proposition. Let me give you a few more.

- *If* a gamma ray burst from a neutron star were to hit the Earth straight on, *then* every living thing on the planet would die.
- *If* the polar ice caps melted completely, *then* sea level would rise 300 feet, completely flooding every coastal city.
- *If* an asteroid the size of Texas were to collide with the Earth, *then* no human being would survive the collision.
- *If* someone were to hold a gigantic, 200 ft. diameter magnifying glass above your head at the exact height of its focal length, and exactly at right angles between you and the sun, *then* you would sizzle and pop just like those ants on the sidewalk when you were a kid.

All of these statements have three things in common. First, they are all "*if / then*" statements. Second, *they are all true*. Thirdly, you're not likely to lose a whole lot of sleep over any one of them because the prerequisite "*if*" portion of each statement is incredibly *unlikely* to happen. People who use really scary statements like these to get you to do something are counting on the scare factor to distract you from examining the "*if*" portion of the statement. Now I'm not suggesting that I'm smarter than Stephen Hawking, and just like all the statements I gave you, his statement is true. My question for him is, does he honestly believe that *no one will be able to solve this problem in the next 584 years?* Can you name any other problem in human history that was still there almost six hundred years later? Humans went from the first airplane flight to landing men on the Moon *in 65 years*, for crying out loud!

But I digress. Back to my original question: How overpopulated is the earth? Well my friends, that is easy to illustrate, and after I do it here, I would not be at all surprised if this is the most under-handed, devious, dirty trick I'm accused of pulling in this book.

Hey, I didn't invent Math.

Grab a calculator and figure along with me if you like. In fact, I'd appreciate you checking my work. First, go to Google and type "Current World Population." When I did that just now, I got 7 Billion. Now, let's gather all those people together in one place. Just for purposes of the illustration, let's give each person four square feet. That's the size of four tiles on your kitchen floor. There would actually be more space between people than they're taking up, and more space than Mr. Hawking envisions for us in 584 years. Yes, I know that's not enough space to live in, but that's not our point here; our point is to vividly illustrate how crowded the Earth is. Now, let's look up how many square feet there are in a square mile. The answer is 27,878,400. Divide that by 4 and you get 6,969,600. So at 4 square feet per person, you can fit 6,969,400 people in a square mile. Now we simply divide 7,000,000,000 by 6,969,400. The answer is (drum roll, please)…. 1,004.36 square miles.

So, if you gathered all of them together in one place, and gave each one four square feet, the resource-depleting, environment-destroying, planet-killing plague that is Humanity would   fill   up….

….the state of Rhode Island, with 204 square miles to spare.

Spiritual….

Spiritual:

1. Of, pertaining to, having the nature of, or consisting of spirit, as distinguished from matter; incorporeal.
2. Pertaining to or affecting the immaterial nature or soul of Man.
3. Of or pertaining to God or to the soul as acted upon by the Holy Spirit; holy; pure.

I find it amusing that people at either extreme of any political or ideological spectrum behave in the exact ways for which they castigate the people at the other end. For example, a major university recently banned all Christmas trees on its campus. The reason: "To promote an air of tolerance." That's right, in the name of *tolerance* they will *no longer tolerate* a Christmas tree.

Scientists and devoutly religious people, who are at opposite ends of a different spectrum, have another thing in common. They both have a very difficult time operating outside their sphere of influence, and yet they feel absolutely compelled to go ahead and do it anyway. When confronted by anyone with diametrically opposing viewpoints, they will immediately try to discredit him or her, no matter how many straws they have to grasp.

Scientists will try to offer a scientific explanation to anything, no matter how absurd it may be, and if they can't explain it scientifically, then they claim it doesn't exist. If someone has an encounter with an unidentified flying flying object, (I know what you're thinking, but hey, it's flying and you can't identify it…. it's a UFO!) the person who actually *had* the experience may say "Well, it was shaped like a giant cigar, 75 feet long, and it had bright green and blue lights blinking along both sides. It came out of the north, did three circles around my ham radio antenna, flew though the hayloft of my neighbor's barn, then took off to the east so fast I could hardly follow it and disappeared behind *that* mountain." The scientist will then confidently offer the only "reasonable" explanation:

"Well, you *obviously* saw the planet Venus."

"But Venus is right over there! I'm pointing at it right now!"

"Swamp gas."

"But we're in the middle of a desert. There isn't a swamp within 500 miles of here."

"Well then......you imagined it."

Similarly, when confronted with fossilized bones of prehistoric animals buried in the ground, some religious zealots will confidently say: "Well, God obviously put them there to fool us and test our faith." (Don't' laugh, I actually heard *that* explanation once.) To me, it makes about as much sense as the idea that we're all really made out of lime Jell-O, but God is only fooling us into thinking that we're flesh and blood.

Saying that you can either believe in science or you can believe in God, but you have to choose one or the other is like saying you can either believe in lipstick, or you believe in dishes, but you can't have it both ways. What people on either side cannot seem to grasp is that there are things in this world that simply lay outside the purview of their philosophy. Theologians cannot help but offer religious explanations for things that have nothing to do with religion, and scientists just can't help trying to offer scientific explanations for things that simply have nothing to do with science.

There are things in this world, which cannot be scientifically proven and never will be. That doesn't mean they don't exist. One of my favorite scenes from the movie Contact, which for those of you who haven't seen it, is one of the best movies ever made about Humanity's first contact with extraterrestrial life, is a scene where Jodie Foster is trying to convince Matthew McConaughey that his spirituality has no validity because it cannot be scientifically proven. Matthew asked her, "Did you love your father?" She says "Of course, very much", to which he replies "Prove it."

When I was in school studying to become a nurse, I took a Developmental Psychology course. I was surprised to learn in class one day that the concept of The Mind is no longer considered valid in psychology. "Don't you need a mind to think?", I asked. "No", the instructor corrected me, "you need a *brain* to think. There is no scientific evidence that there is such a thing as the Mind or a soul for that matter." You know what? I'm fine with that statement, in a *Science* class. I have no problem with scientists observing and following the scientific method. I expect scientists to go by the evidence and nothing but the evidence without letting any personal feelings or pressure from any interested parties get in the way. If they stopped doing that, science would be useless, and it could not have contributed all the things it has to the betterment of the world. What annoys me is when scientists stop investigating the unexplained and start *explaining the uninvestigated.*

I attended all the classes. I answered the questions on all of the tests correctly (well, enough of them anyway) and passed the course with an A, but I never really believed what the instructor said that day. I still don't believe it. I can believe the brain is the seat of thought and consciousness, but I don't believe that the electrical impulses in my brain are *all that I am.*

There is more to me than my brain. There is more to *you* than *your* brain. We have spirits. We have souls. Those souls came from somewhere, and for me, the best explanation I can find is a supreme being. I can't prove it, and I have absolutely no stake in anyone else believing it, I'm just sharing a personal opinion.

I'm in good company in this respect. Some sort of animistic belief; belief in a spiritual component to reality, has been common to the vast majority of human cultures from the beginning of human consciousness. Today, 95% of all humans believe in some sort of a supreme being. That supreme being is called a lot of different things in a lot of different cultures. In this culture we call it God.

So why do I believe that God exists? I believe God exists because his existence explains so many things that just don't make sense any other way. Science tells us the "how" of the universe but it cannot touch the "why." If you ask, "How do I exist?", A biologist can tell you all about anatomy, physiology, chemistry, and biology, but if you ask him "Why do I exist?", the scientist has nothing to say. If he's an arrogant scientist, he'll tell you "There is no reason why you exist, you just do. Some primordial soup spontaneously generated life a billion years ago, and here you are. There is no reason." For me, that just doesn't cut it. It is totally unsatisfactory. There are so many better answers that scientist could have given. How about "I don't know", or "Well, here's where we depart from science, but here's what I think", or "Here's what I believe."

There's a distinction between saying "I believe in the existence of God", and "I have faith God." Faith is belief without need of proof. Personally, I don't need faith in the existence of God because I see *evidence* of his existence all around me. For me, the very fact that I exist, that I am, that I think, that I feel, that I love, is evidence of God's existence.

I think what a person believes lies at the intersection of what they *want* to believe, what they *need* to believe, and what they are *able to* believe, and when I listen to explanations of the universe without purpose, without a reason for its existence, and that life is nothing more then the random interactions of elements over time, I am simply *unable* to believe it. There are people who would have me believe that what I perceive as myself is nothing more than the electrical patterns of neurons firing in my brain. They can believe that if they want to, but I cannot. It's not that I refuse to consider that possibility; it's that I'm *unable* to believe it. I've tried plugging that idea into my schema and it won't stick. It just pops right out again, falls on the floor and rolls off into a corner. For me, the existence of *existence* is most easily and satisfying explained by the existence of God. I know I've been arguing the case for reason and critical thinking and expecting people to be able to support their argument with logic and empirical evidence, and I know in this case I have none to offer. I'm going strictly on my feelings, but I'm not presenting those feelings as the basis for expecting anyone else to change their behavior, so you see, in *this one case*, that really *does* make everything okay.

For me, another convincing piece of evidence for the existence of God is beauty. I'm talking about *unnecessary* beauty; beauty that doesn't really *need* to be there, but is. I'm talking about the beauty of the Rocky Mountains in the fall, with the aspen trees almost glowing with their own inner light. I'm talking about the beauty of a thunderstorm towering over the emptiness of the Great Plains. I'm talking about the beauty of the sunset over the Pacific Ocean. These things don't serve any discernable purpose; they just are, and yet they have a profound effect on people. Well okay, they have a profound effect on *me*. To suggest that this is nothing more than a particular pattern of neurons firing in a particular sequence is to me, absurd. What could possibly be the evolutionary imperative in that?

I have a collection of seashells at my house that I've been slowly accumulating for the last 20 years. I have a few hundred of them now, and I have several books depicting thousands more. There is astounding variety; Cowries, Whelks, Sundials, Harp Shells, Top Shells, Conchs, Limpets, Cone Shells, Olive Shells, and with a few exceptions, I find all of them to be beautiful. Why? They all have basically the same purpose, to protect the soft body of the animal inside. One drab, unremarkable design would do the job, so why all the variety, and all the beauty? To me, seashells are God's doodles.

How about the beauty of art? I'm not talking modern art, I'm talking *real* art; the kind of art no one seems to have the talent to produce anymore. Music, sculpture, literature, architecture, none of these things are *necessary* for the continuance of life, and yet there are examples of each that can move millions of people to tears. Why? While we're at it, let's not forget physical human beauty. That's a little easier to explain in terms of an evolutionary imperative. We are drawn to the beauty of the opposite sex so that we will reproduce, but to reduce the excitement, the appreciation and the affirmation of life that I feel at the site of a beautiful woman to nothing more then an inducement to pump out replacements is just downright depressing. Even if it could be reduced to that, it begs the question: *Why* do we reproduce? When it comes down to it, *why* should life go on? These are the questions science can't even touch.

By the way, if I give the impression that I don't believe in evolution, let me put that to rest right now. Actually, to say that I *believe in* evolution implies that I have faith that evolution is going to do something for me. It's more accurate to say that I believe evolution occurs. I can find no contradiction between the existence of evolution and the existence of God. I love to listen to arguments against evolution because none I've ever heard could stand up to one minute of logic or reason.

One of my favorites is: "If evolution is real, how come it's still just a theory?" During my first attempt at college I majored in music, and several of my classes were about.... Music Theory! Does that mean no one's ever proven that music exists? Later in my life, while I was training to become a pilot, I studied....*Aerodynamic* Theory! Can we conclude that no one's ever proven that airplanes can fly? Like a lot of words in the English language, the word "theory" has several meanings, one of which is "An integrated group of fundamental principles underlying a science or its practical applications." *This* is where the term "Evolutionary Theory" comes from.

If anyone tells you that the Theory of Evolution denies the existence of God, they're either lying to you, or they don't understand the Theory of Evolution. Here's what the theory *actually says:*

1. Due to predation, there are many more individuals born in each generation of organisms, than will live to adulthood.

2. In each generation, there are small genetic variations between individuals. (Has there been any statement that God doesn't exist yet? If there was, I sure missed it.)
3. Every once in a while, one of those variations will be advantageous to that individual; it will make it less likely to die or be eaten before it can reproduce. Those variations will be passed on to the genome of the next generation. (Any denial of God's existence there? Nope, let's move on.)
4. After many generations, the advantageous variations that are passed on will accumulate one on top of another, until the organism is no longer the same organism, but a new species.

Now, did the words "There is no God" appear anywhere in what I've just written? No. There is no contradiction between believing that evolution occurs and believing in God, nor can any scientific experiment ever be devised that could disprove God's existence. It cannot be done. One of the difficulties with evolution is, it's impossible for us to conceptualize the vast time scales over which it operates. We're talking tens of millions of generations of living things over billions of years. Do any of us really have any concept of how long *two hundred* years is, let alone one million?

If you've ever studied Anatomy and Physiology, you have some idea of how incredibly complicated the human body is. For that matter, any single living cell is an incredible piece of machinery. I used to see a cell as just kind of a little bag of soup, with molecules occasionally bumping into each other and lazily interacting to produce something the cell could use. Nothing could be further from the truth. A cell carries on its business with blinding speed. There are little enzyme factories in there pumping out perfect copies of thousands of different molecules as fast as *50,000 times a second.* It is every bit as complicated a mechanism as a nuclear submarine. If we were walking along the beach one day and came across one of *those* washed up on the shore, would you take a look at it and say, "Well, this obviously spontaneously assembled itself from primeval elements." If you did, I would look at you askance, to say the least. I must conclude that something *that* complicated and whose millions of parts are so interdependent upon each other to make it work *must* have been *designed.* A living cell, let alone the whole animal, is every bit as complicated, and interdependent as a nuclear submarine, so why is it so hard to believe that the cell was designed as well?

While we're on the subject of designing things, consider this. If you had the skill to sit down and design a nuclear submarine, right down to the last nut, bolt, circuit and seam, that's still all you would have; a *design*. Someone still has to go out and *build* the damned thing. Could it not be that God is the designer and evolution is the manufacturing process? I mean really, if you were a supreme being, and you had eternity to spend on a project, would you wrap the whole thing up in six days, or would you play with it a while, tweak it here and there, set it loose and see what happens, and then tinker some more? I don't think God likes being bored.

There is one last piece of evidence for God that I've been saving for last, and that is the atom. Hopefully we all learned in school that atoms are the most basic building blocks of all matter, but all atoms are built out of the same parts: protons, neutrons and electrons. Every element in the universe is made up of different numbers of these same three particles. The nucleus of an atom is made up of different numbers of protons and neutrons, but it's the electrons that I find really interesting. The electrons orbit around the nucleus in different layers or shells. There is room in the first shell for two electrons. The second will hold six, the third will hold ten, the fourth fourteen, the fifth eighteen, and so on. The number of protons and neutrons in the nucleus and the number of electrons orbiting in their shells determine what element the atom is. Each shell wants to have its maximum number of electrons in it. If they're there, the atom will go ahead and start another shell. If they're not, the atom will try to steal the missing electrons from another atom, or the two atoms will share them. Believe it or not, stealing and sharing electrons is the whole basis of chemistry. Every chemical reaction, living or not, is nothing more than that.

Now consider those electron shells again. If you didn't already notice it, there is a pattern to their maximum capacity. The number of electrons that can fit into each shell increases by four with each successive shell. It does not increase by some random number from atom to atom, but exactly four every single time, no more, no less, ever. It is the same for every element in existence. As far as we know, you could travel to the other end of the universe, and you would still find every single atom constructed in exactly the same way. If they weren't, nothing in the universe would work; the laws of chemistry and physics wouldn't exist. There would be nothing but chaos. I once pointed that out to someone who I'm guessing was an atheist, and without so much as a second's consideration, he nonchalantly replied, "Yes, evolution can often appear to be order emerging from chaos, but that's all it is, an *appearance*." Excuse me, but to the best of my or anyone else's knowlege....

....*atoms don't evolve.*

If they did, and the laws of chemistry would be continually changing, and the universe really would be nothing but chaos. Oxygen atoms, iron atoms, carbon atoms, plutonium atoms; they're all exactly the same now as they were a twelve billion years ago. As a matter of fact, *they're the same atoms!*

Any and every atom you care to examine is representative of every other atom of that element anywhere in the universe. The definition of a pattern is "A representative, regular or intelligible form", so the identical construction of each and every atom fits the definition of a *pattern*. The definition of "Design" is: "An intelligent, purposeful or discoverable *pattern*, as opposed to chaos." Atoms make up everything you see; the entire universe as we know it, and it works very, very well. The universe, right down to its most fundamental unit, is the very essence of design, which begs the question: who is the designer?

I know there are several different definitions of these words, someone else might use other equally valid definitions to reach a completely different conclusion. I really don't care. I certainly don't expect to change anyone's mind on either side of this argument, but I've satisfied myself that the universe was designed and created by a purposeful, intelligent supreme being whom I choose to call God, and I did it with some simple logic, common knowledge, a community college Anatomy and Physiology course, and the Readers Digest Great Encyclopedic Dictionary. Hey, I didn't write the dictionary, I just quoted it. If you don't like my dictionary, take it up with Readers Digest. When it comes down to it, I wrote this chapter every bit as much for me as I wrote it for you. If you're able to take something positive from it, great. If not, that's okay too. We're good either way.

But Not Religious

First off I'd like to emphasize that this is not, and I repeat *not* an essay about why you should hold or not hold any particular religious faith. I'm not writing it to attack or cast doubt on anyone's faith, but simply to explain my own position, and to let anyone else out there who might feel the same way know that they are not evil, they are not crazy, and they are not alone. If your faith is strong, I'm not going to be able to damage it anyway. Nor am I singling out Christianity, I just happen to have been born in United States, which is and always has been a predominantly Christian nation. If I had been born in India, I would be writing the same things about Hinduism. If I had been born in Southeast Asia I'd be writing the same things about Buddhism. If I had been born somewhere in a Muslim country, I just might have my head lopped off with a sword for what I'm about to say. That's just another reason I'm grateful to be an American.

When I was growing up, my family didn't go to church. I really don't remember the first time I ever asked one of my parents who God was or what they said, but I'm sure I did, and I'm sure they said something. I think the lack of religion in our house was probably my late father's influence. He is no longer around to discuss the issue, but as far as I can figure, he was somewhere between an agnostic and an atheist. I remember once during a disagreement with him, I mentioned something about my soul, and he said *"There's no scientific proof that there is any such thing as a soul!"* Well, you already know my position on that subject from the previous chapter, so I have extrapolated in my own mind where my father stood on the subject. As far as I know, my mother has always been a Christian.

I didn't really have any exposure to religion until I was nine years old, when my father started taking my brother, my sister and me to an Episcopal church in Denver. My sister asked him not long after that what an Episcopalian was, to which we he replied with a perfectly deadpan expression that an Episcopalian was a person who goes around pissing in pails. Personally, I always preferred the definition of an Episcopalian as "A Catholic who flunked Latin." I always found it a little puzzling that it was my father and not my mother who was the first to expose us kids to religion, but now I'm sure it was an attempt after their divorce to prove that he was a good and worthy parent. Either that, or it was somewhere in the divorce agreement. Whatever the motivation, it only lasted a couple of years. I don't know if it was a conscious decision to stop attending, or if it just kind of fell by the wayside out of a lack of real conviction on my father's part.

Having grown up in a Christian country, attending only Christian churches, however sporadically, and learning that I was actually baptized as an Episcopalian, I just always assumed that I was a Christian, so it was always vaguely disturbing to me that I was never completely comfortable in a church, and it took me a long, long time to figure out why.

I'm assuming that somewhere along the line, probably in Sunday School, I was introduced to the doctrine of original sin, which said that I was a sinner whether I wanted to be or not, no matter what I did, no matter how good I tried to be. I think that's where it started, because deep down in my heart, I didn't believe it. Something about it just didn't ring true. I didn't *feel* like a bad person. In fact, I can honestly say that at no time in my whole young life did I ever intentionally do anything I knew to be wrong. My family may not have been churchgoers in my formative years, but my parents did an excellent job of teaching me about right and wrong, so in Sunday school, it was like being accused, tried and convicted of something I hadn't done. To me, there was no justice in that, and yet speaking out about it didn't seem like a good idea at all.

So that was it. I was a *bad* Christian. I was a bad Christian because I didn't believe what God had said, and how can a child be expected to mount a credible defense against *that* kind of charge? There was no way out. I was caught in a vicious cycle. I was a bad Christian because I didn't believe Christian doctrine, and I didn't believe Christian doctrine because I was a bad Christian. What was worse was that I was sitting there in church and Sunday school, surrounded by all those people who *did* believe. What if they found out I wasn't one of them? Would they one day all stand up, point me and start letting out those weird screams, like the pod people in Invasion of the Body Snatchers? Of course, I describe all of this with 45 years of hindsight. I didn't have the vocabulary or the perspective to express it then.

As an adult, sometime in my late 30's or early 40's as far as I can tell, I went through a sort of philosophical awakening. I'm not sure exactly what set it off, but I began to look at different aspects of life, set aside everything I'd ever been taught about them, and start asking questions; lots and lots of questions, tough questions, often brutal questions. I basically tried to tear down my own understanding of the world with the biggest gun I could find to see what would be left standing. I looked at the pieces of the rubble and tried to see how each of them aligned with what I objectively knew to be true, what made sense, and what stood up to reason. Whenever a piece failed to measure up, I threw it out. When I started thinking about a subject I tried to look at it from every angle and most of all, question the assumptions I had always followed about it. Instead of asking "Why is this so?", I'd ask "*Is it really so, or is it just what I've always been told?* I was astonished at how often that turned out to be the case, and I eventually concluded that if you'll begin with the assumption that most of what you *thought* you knew is wrong, you have a pretty good start.

I found that once I started down this road, it was hard to hit the brakes. Pillar after pillar of society and civilization fell under my philosophical jackhammer, and I realized it was only a matter of time before I couldn't avoid religion any longer. One day, I took a deep breath and started with everything that really bothered me about it.

Whenever I thought about religion, I didn't feel comfort or peace, I felt tension and unease. I felt especially uncomfortable in church, because there, I secretly knew that I was a fraud. Correction: *God* and I knew that I was a fraud. Yep, that pretty much summed it up. That's the pickle I'd been in most of my life.

But now it was time to dig deep and see if it was really that simple.

I felt uncomfortable in church. Well what is a church? It's a building where people worship God. Was I uncomfortable with the building, with the people, or with God? The building is just building; an inanimate object. That wasn't it. The people? Well, there *is* that Invasion of the Body Snatchers thing. That can really be scary to think about especially when you're nine years old. Was it God I was uncomfortable with? Let's see, an invisible, omnipresent, all-powerful being with the ability and, if I believed some people, the inclination to throw me in a lake of fire for all eternity. Bingo! We have a winner! But why would God want to do that to *me*. I was just a kid. Would he really do that just because I didn't believe what others in church believed?

After all, it was right there in the Bible. But how do we know the Bible is true? Because it's the word of God. But how do we know it's the word of God? Because it says so in the Bible? And how do we *know* the Bible is true? *Because it's the word of God.* How do we *know* that? Because it's in the Bible.... and so on, and so on until someone loses their patience and says "You just have to have faith!' Well, okay....*how do I get that?*

Why didn't I have faith? What was it that made me unable to believe without question? Well there are several reasons, and with your indulgence, I'm going to present a series of thought experiments to illustrate each one. I know I've talked about throwing out assumptions, but I'm going to start with one that I think will be acceptable to just about every spiritual person. I'm going to start with the assumption that God is perfect and people are imperfect. I think if you're going to believe in God at all, that's a pretty standard viewpoint. So let's take a look at several of the things that God has supposedly set up for us in the Bible.

First of all, there's Hell. Whether you like it or not, no matter how uncomfortable it makes you, or even whether you believe in it or not, Hell is one of the tenets of Christianity. You have to deal with it in one way or another. (I'm amazed now at how many good Christians don't believe in Hell at all. Actually, the Bible says almost nothing about Hell. We actually get most of our ideas about it from Dante's Inferno, but I didn't know any of this back then.)

Of course, the idea behind Hell is punishment for doing wrong, and that may be a good idea, but no matter how much I look at it, Hell is taking a good idea way too far. If you have a child, you want that child to be healthy and safe, and you want them to grow up to be a good person. That means disciplining them when they go astray. What is your motivation? Is it simply retribution, or is it to guide them away from behaviors that are going to decrease their happiness and prosperity, and toward behaviors that are going to increase them? Hellfire and brimstone Christians will tell you that Hell serves the exact same purpose, but can anyone tell me the purpose of an *eternal* punishment? The reason we punish our children when they do wrong is so that they won't do it again. If we never give them a chance *not* to do it again, the point of the punishment is lost. If your child does repeat those same harmful behaviors even after they've been warned not to, is it then proper to beat them with a belt every minute of the rest of their existence? Why not? After all, they were warned beforehand. Our society would never tolerate that kind of abuse; we put people who do that sort of thing in prison. But forget society, *we don't subject our children to cruel torture **because we love them.*** So how does it work out that God, whose love for us is supposedly infinite, does exactly that? It just didn't fit.

Let's look at it from a purely pragmatic point of view. How many people do you think are in Hell right now? Hundreds? Thousand? Millions? If Hell is not only a punishment for sin, but also a *deterrent* for those of us who have not yet earned damnation, then by anyone's measure, *Hell is a miserable failure.* How can a perfect God be the creator of something so pathetically *imperfect?*

Of course those same hellfire and brimstone Christians will also tell you that no one *has* to go to hell. It's a choice we all make, because God wants us to have free will.

Ah yes, free will. Let's look at that for a minute. Here's the next thought experiment. Let's say you come over to my house for lunch one day and find that I fixed you two lunches. One is a nice healthy salad, and the other is a big greasy cheeseburger that will clog your arteries before you even finish eating it. I tell you that I fixed both of these because I want you to have a choice. Then I pull out a 357-magnum revolver from underneath the table and tell you that I love you and I want you to have a long happy healthy life, so if you choose the cheeseburger, I'm going to blow your brains out.... *But,* you still have a *choice.* Of course I wouldn't really do that, would I? That cheeseburger looks awfully good, you start to reach for it, and I cock the hammer on the revolver. You look at me again and I mouth the words "love you" with a completely angelic smile on my face. Would you think I was a completely stable person at that moment? Would you still reach for the cheeseburger? The truth is, I *haven't* given you a choice, and you'd think I was patently insane.

Free will with the sentence of the eternal damnation for ever using it **is not free will!** To say that is to insist that every prisoner in Hitler's concentration camps was as free as a bird. They were perfectly free to walk over to that fence and try to climb it anytime they wanted. Any decent person would put anyone who made that claim in the same category with those who deny the Holocaust ever happened, and yet we ascribe this reasoning to God, who's justice is infinite?

Let's talk about Satan. Christian doctrine maintains that Satan was once an angel, one of God's servants. Well he ain't anymore, so why does God put up with him? If God's power is infinite, then he could wipe Satan out of existence with a single thought, so why doesn't he do that?

Again, another thought experiment: Suppose you have a nice house, a loving spouse and ten wonderful children. You also have a horrible, hideous, bloodthirsty fanged monster lurking outside your house, intent on ripping your children to shreds and just waiting for someone to leave a door or a window open. (Hey, I never said my thought experiments wouldn't involve some suspension of disbelief. It makes for better movies, and it makes for more effective thought experiments.) Now the question is, do you go merrily about your daily routine, reading the newspaper and drinking a cup of coffee, oblivious to the screams of your children as seven of them are ripped limb from limb and devoured? Do you hand a gun to the other three of them and tell them *their* job is to protect their siblings, or do you **go outside and kill the monster?** You kill the monster, of course, because any parent worthy of the title protects their children from harm, no exceptions, no ifs, ands, or buts.

Why the monster metaphor, and why do I specify *seven* kids eaten by the monster? The Bible says that only Christians go to heaven; "I am the way and the light. No one comes to the father but through me." Again, this is Christian doctrine, I didn't make it up, and you may not like it, but that's the way it is. 70% of the people on Earth are *not* Christians. According to Christian doctrine, they will never make it to Heaven, and evidently, God is fine with that. Listen, I want my son to have free will too, but I don't let him hang around in the middle of the highway, yet I am supposed to believe that God will stand by and let *most* of his children, all of whom he loves, burn in the fires of hell for all eternity. I'm sorry, but I'm just not buying it.

While we're delving into parents and children, let me ask you this: Do you *tell* your children you love them? Do you maintain a presence in their lives and tell them you love them face-to-face every day? Or, do you write it on a note and leave it for them to find, never bother to show up at home, and let them go their entire life without ever seeing your face? It's okay, you're still a good Parent right? After all, you *did* leave them a note, right?

Several times in my life, I've had people try to show me the light. They tell me how much God loves me and that he has a plan for my life. The last few times it happened, I've asked them:

"Why am I hearing this from *you*? Why am I not hearing it from *God*? Why is he not telling me himself?"

"Well, God *is* telling you himself, through me."

"Mmmmmmm…yeah, not quite good enough."

"Excuse me?" (Eyebrow raised…)

"Yeah, you see, listen to this: "Himself……*though you. Himself…..through you.* Do you hear a *little bit* of a difference there?"

(eyebrow raised, hands on hips…) "So what do you want?

"I want God to tell me, out loud, with sound waves traveling through the air and hitting my eardrums."

"You mean you want God to talk to you, audibly, personally? Like he did to Abraham, or Noah?"

"Yeah, now you've got it!"

(Eyebrows raised, hands on hips, weight shifted to one leg…) "So you want a *miracle?*"

"If that's what you want to call it, yes."

"You know, some things have to be believed to be seen."

"And some things are so obvious that it's crazy to deny them. If a big crack opens up in the ground ahead of me, I don't have to *believe* it to fall in; it's *there.*" Why doesn't God make it that obvious, not only to me, but to everyone?

(Arms crossed, one toe tapping, tongue being bitten…) "How can you be so flippant about this? What on Earth makes you think you're deserving of that when you're not even a believer?"

"Does God love me as much as he loved Abraham or Noah?"

"Yes, of course."

"Is my soul at stake?"

"Yes, it is."

"Then why on Earth would he **not** want to tell me himself? For him, it would be like blinking his eyes."

(Weary sigh) "Well, don't worry, you're not the first to question God. He loves you anyway."

"You don't get it, do you? I'm not questioning God. God never told me any of the things I question. They were *all* told to me by *people*, like you. So you see, I'm not questioning *God*, I'm questioning *you.*"

It's really what it all came down to. I was told all these things about God that just didn't make sense to me. I was told he does things that, were I to do them, I would be at best be ostracized and at worst put in prison. In order to believe what I was supposedly told by an infinitely wise and just deity,   (but was *actually* told by people) I would have to throw reason, logic and justice out the window. If God created everything, he created logic and reason too. I did not subscribe to strict, litoral Christian doctrine because to do so would have required me to except a lower standard of behavior from God then any real Christian would ever accept from me, and I couldn't do that. I don't care what anyone says, God is *better* than us.

People would ask me "How can you believe in God and not believe in religion?" That question assumes that religion came from God, and I didn't make that assumption either. I couldn't reconcile the imperfections in religion with a divine origin. The only way I could make religion work would have been with the universal patch of faith; belief without need of proof. Don't question it, just believe it, because we don't have the answers you want, and God won't give them to you. Why would God withhold proof? My answer: He *wouldn't.* I could either ascribe all those grossly imperfect doctrines to a perfect God, or to imperfect people. Guess which one I chose.

You'll notice that I've been using the past tense. That's because these days, I don't worry about it; I'm at peace with it. I realize that the vast majority of all Christians I've ever known are good, nice people, and making me uncomfortable is the last thing they want to do. Occasionally, someone will still try to lead me to the light, and I've come up with a response that seems to work. I simply tell them my position on the matter, and I invite them to jump right in the second I say anything they disagree with, or they think I've gotten just plain wrong. So far, none of them have. I tell them this:

God is omniscient and omnipotent. He is all-seeing, all-knowing, all-powerful. So God...the Almighty...the Great I Am, ...the Supreme Creator of the infinite universe.... doesn't really *need* [insert your name here] to *speak for him*. Anything God wants to communicate to me, he is supremely capable of communicating to me directly, without any intermediaries whatsoever. All I have to do is open my mind and listen, and I do that at least a dozen times a day. If God wants me to live my life in any particular way, I have every confidence he'll do just that, and if he has not *yet* chosen to do that, I can only take that as evidence that I'm getting it mostly right already. Don't you agree?

It's very interesting that as soon as I say "Don't you agree?" There's almost always just a second's hesitation on their part. It makes me wonder sometimes who really has *more faith....*

....them, or me.

The Separation of Church and State

I had a tough time starting this chapter. I realized last night that I had only four months left if I wanted to meet my goal of getting this book before the public by the end of the year, so I was feeling a little desperate. I thought I was going to knock it out in a couple of days, but it looks like that's not going to happen. Sometimes when you start spouting things off the top of your head, (as opposed to spouting things *out* of the top of your head, I guess), you find that you're not quite as eloquent as you thought you were, and your points aren't going to be nearly as strong as they could be without some concrete, real world examples. So, I started to do a little research.

One of the first things I came across was actually the Universal Declaration of Human Rights adopted by the United Nations in 1948. Part of this document states: "Everyone has the right to freedom of thought, conscience and religion; this right includes freedom to change his religion or belief *and freedom, either alone or in community with others and **in public** or private*, to manifest his religion or belief in teaching, practice, worship and observance."

Now I'm not a fan of any organization that thinks it supersedes, or at least would *like* to supersede the sovereign government to my country, but even a broken clock is right twice a day. Do me a favor and read it again, focusing on the italicized part. Keep in mind that this is not from a bunch of radical right wing fanatics; this is from the *United Nations*. I'm assuming that when they use the word "everyone", they are including Americans, so I find it very curious that what the United Nations hath given, a lot of Americans are trying very hard to take away.

I also visited the "State/Church FAQ page of the Freedom From Religion Foundation's website. I found questions like these:

- The school board in my district is praying before school board meetings. Is that legal?
- A church is being used as a polling location. Is that legal?
- A store in my neighborhood is offering a discount or promotion for bringing in a church bulletin. Is that legal?
- My child's school choir is singing religious music. Is that legal?
- A church is participating in political lobbying. What can I do about it?

Not surprisingly, the FFRF assured inquirers that *all* of these things are very *illegal*. For religious activities to be legal, they must be carried out in private, out of view of the public. And from whence does the FFRF claim this legal authority comes? As it turns out, it comes from the United States Constitution, specifically the First Amendment in the Bill of Rights. So, on the one hand, we have the *United Nations* telling us that we have the *right* to observe and practice our religion in public, and on the other we have the *Constitution* telling us that to do so is *illegal?* Could it actually be that our Constitution is in direct violation of the United Nations Universal Declaration of Human Rights?

Now I'm doing some speculating here, I'll admit that. I may be flat out wrong, and if you'd like to come up with some solid evidence that I am, I'll retract my opinion. I've done it before. I'll wager the *same people* who are big fans of the United Nations, consider it a defender of human rights around the world, hold it as a legitimate authority over the conduct of human affairs, and wholeheartedly endorse its declaration that *everyone* has the right to manifest their religious beliefs *in public*, are the very same people who will, at the drop of a hat, cite the Constitution as the source of their authority to prevent people from doing exactly that in this country. I find it very curious that the people who run straight to the First Amendment of the Constitution and steadfastly cling to it as the undeniable and unquestionable authority for their argument, are the same people who will tell you that the very next amendment, from the very same document has no validity whatsoever. But, that's another discussion.

With all of the controversy surrounding religious freedom and government these days, you might get the impression that there are whole paragraphs devoted to it in the Bill of Rights. You'd be wrong. The First Amendment contains exactly sixteen words on the subject. I'll put up $100 that says if you were to ask a hundred people on the street what the First Amendment says, three quarters of them couldn't tell you at all. (I personally know one woman who thought the Constitution itself was "every law that's ever been passed." I'm glad to say she now knows that what she was thinking of is actually the Federal Register, not the Constitution, but it just goes to show you how bad the situation is.) The other twenty-five people might be able to tell you "Congress shall make no law respecting an establishment of religion" and anyone listening in would say "Oh yeah, that's it. Now I remember." But wait a minute…. I said sixteen words; that's only ten. I must be wrong, huh?

The exact wording of the First Amendment actually is: *"Congress shall make no law respecting an establishment of religion, or prohibiting the free exercise thereof; or abridging the freedom of speech, or of the press; or the right of the people peaceably to assemble, and to petition the government for a redress of grievances."*

So, the missing words are "or prohibiting the free exercise thereof." How convenient that *those* words are so often left out. Still, those first ten words are right there in plain English, right? So what's the problem?

The problem is, the constitution is written in *18th-century* English. Languages evolve over time. If they didn't, you and I would still be speaking Proto-Indo-European. They don't evolve abruptly, (well, unless you count up-speak and substituting numbers 4 words) but by tiny little changes in usage. A few of those have taken place since the Constitution was written. In this case, the whole problem; the source of all the hullabaloo about the separation of church and state in America today stems from just five words: "respecting an establishment of religion."

In 21st Century English, most people would interpret that as "Paying respect to a religious establishment", as in a church. That is inaccurate. Like a lot of words in our overly complicated, messed up language, the word "respect" has more than one definition. When we hear it, we tend to automatically think of the first definition; "A feeling of deep admiration." However, the second definition is "A particular aspect, point or detail", as in "In this aspect" = "Regarding this detail" = "In this respect." So, where people in the 18th century would use the word "respecting", people in the 21st-century usually say "With respect to." I'm not exactly sure when the change in usage took place, but the older expression "Respecting" is still found in the Fugitive Slave Act of 1850. What can I say; people in the 18th century were big on participles. When you see the two examples side-by-side, you can easily see that they mean the same thing. We don't use participles this way a lot today, but it's still proper usage of English, and you have to remember, the men who wrote the constitution literally *were Englishmen.*

On to the next word, and no, I don't mean "an." An is an article, and articles are the most unsexy, uninteresting words there are. The word "establishment" in the First Amendment is *not a noun* but actually the noun form of the verb "to establish." Believe it or not, that's an important difference. If you're using the verb form of nouns, then where buildings have been constructed, there has been *a construction* of buildings. When words are pronounced, there has been *a pronunciation* of words. Where a system has been corrupted, there has been a *corruption* of that system. Where an area has been populated, there has been *a population* of that area. Are you starting to get the hang of it? Again, we don't use the noun form of verbs a lot, we just use the verb, but the way we use English today does not change the meaning of what people said in the past.

So what did they actually say? If you translate the Establishment Clause of the First Amendment into 21st century English, here's what you get:

Congress shall make no law with respect to the establishment of a religion, or prohibiting the free exercise thereof.

There is no secret code. There is no need to decipher an archaic and half forgotten dialect. The Constitution is not a first draft. The framers of the Constitution did not set out to craft a document that only future lawyers, scholars, linguists or Supreme Court justices would be able to interpret. They wrote it in the common language of the day, for anyone and everyone to read and understand. It says what it means and it means what it says. The government shall not establish a state religion and compel you to follow it, and the government shall not prohibit you from *freely* exercising any religion, or no religion at all if that is what you choose. In other words *the government shall keep its big fat nose out of yours and everyone else's religious business.*

I try not to rehash what other people have said, but in this case it bears repeating. The separation of church and state is not to protect the government and the people from religion, but *to protect religion from the government.* Does that sound like what's happening today? What *has* happened is, what was designed as a benign acceptance of all religion has been twisted and perverted into the systematic suppression of one.

But if it really is as simple as I've explained it here, then why has there been so much controversy? Why have there been lawsuits that reached all the way to the Supreme Court, and why did the Supreme Court spend so much time and effort "interpreting" something I claim needs no interpretation? Am I actually suggesting that I understand something that the smartest people in our judicial system just don't get?

No, I am not. They understand everything I'm telling you here, just as clearly as I do, and just as clearly as you do now. They know the First Amendment protects the rights of the people to freely exercise their religion openly and without fear of coercion or suppression from the government. So why have they "interpreted" the First Amendment in ways so far reaching and intrusive into peoples lives? Well, I don't know how to soften this.

I don't know how to sugarcoat it, or pussyfoot around it. They did it because *they could.* They had the power, and they had a political agenda. There you go.

Let me ask another question. What is the only, and I mean the *only* entity mentioned in the Establishment Clause? Is it the attendees of a high school football game or graduation? Is it the local school board? Is it Mrs. Potter's third-grade class? No, it's **Congress** *and no one else.* The Establishment Clause of the First Amendment is a clear, concise prohibition against Congress, *and that's all it is.* Therefore, Congress is the *only* entity that can violate it.

- A Town Council praying before their meeting is not violating the First Amendment *because they are not Congress.*
- Students praying in school are not violating the First Amendment, *because they are not Congress.*
- Their school allowing them to pray is not violating the First Amendment, *because it is not Congress.*
- A town council putting up a nativity scene in their Town square are not violating the First Amendment, *because they are not Congress.*
- A courthouse displaying the 10 Commandments on its front lawn is not violating the First Amendment, *because the people who put it there are not Congress.*
- The president or members of Congress attending the National Prayer Breakfast in Washington DC each February are not violating the First Amendment, *because they are not there to pass a law establishing a religion.*
- The Senate or House of Representatives opening a legislative session with a prayer are not violating the First Amendment, *because they are not making a law establishing a state religion.*

In fact, since Congress has never passed a law establishing a state religion, the Establishment Clause of the First Amendment has never actually been violated in the entire history of the United States. What has happened is much, much worse…. people have been *offended!*

To be more precise, people have been made uncomfortable, and they have sought to eliminate the things that make them uncomfortable. They have interpreted "freedom from religion" to mean the right to never be exposed to it. They would probably say "be forced to partake in it", but in fact people in this country are not forced to participate in any religion, any more than vegetarians watching a cooking show about grilling steaks are being *forced* to eat meat, or people standing on the street when a Gay Pride parade passes by are being *forced* to change their sexual orientation. Since 83% of Americans still identify themselves as Christians, the people who are being made uncomfortable by religion are a small minority. Tell me, if 17% of the spectators at a gay pride parade were uncomfortable with it, should the parade be canceled? Are any of the organizers of the parade going to champion *those people's* right to never be made uncomfortable? So you see, it really is a perfectly okay to offend people and make them uncomfortable, as long as you're offending the *right* people.

I know a young man who is not only uncomfortable with religion, but openly hostile to it. He has reposted memes on Facebook referring to Christians in ways that I simply refuse to repeat here, knowing full well that his mother and sister are both devout Christians. At family reunions, when a blessing is being said before the meal, he leans against a counter, crosses his arms and scowls at the floor in front of him.

What he might be surprised to learn is, I completely understand his discomfort. He is made terribly uncomfortable by religion because he does not want people he did not choose telling him how to live his life or impinging on his personal sovereignty or freedom. Now does that sound vaguely familiar? I also do not want to people I did not choose telling me how to live my life or impinging on my personal sovereignty and freedom, only the institution I'm referring to is not religion, but the Federal Government and for that, he and his peers think I'm a certifiable nut case.

Here's what I'd like to point out to him, and to anyone who feels compelled to try to erase religion from American culture: In the United States, *because of* the First Amendment, adherence to any religion is completely voluntary. No one, other than perhaps your parents, can *ever* force you to go to church, or to pray at a football game, or to say a blessing before a meal. Adherence to the federal government on the other hand, is anything *but* voluntary. The government has armed police, and SWAT teams in armored vehicles, and prisons surrounded by razor wire to force you to comply with what they tell you to do.

So my question for them is: Who actually has *more* power to *force* you to live in any particular way; the preacher down at the Methodist Church, or the Federal Government?

So why am *I* the nut case?

Gay Marriage

This one is simple. On the one side, we have gay people, who only want the right to enter into committed and legally recognized marriages with the people they love. On the other side, we have the Mean, bigoted, homophobic Christian Right Wingers who hate gay people for being who they are and want to punish them, Right?

Well yes, and no.

This might be how it appears to someone who cannot be bothered to look any deeper than the surface of the issue, or apply any critical thinking to it. Are there some Christian Right Wingers who just plain hate gay people and want them punished? Of course there are. Any group that has 1.09 billion members is going to have a few rotten apples. But, there are a great many more people whose concern about gay marriage has very little to do with sexual orientation and very much to do with the definition of *family,* and to them, one man, married to one woman, and their biological offspring; in other words the traditional nuclear family, *is* the definition of that word.

Now, I'm well aware that it's terribly politically incorrect to suggest that any one type of family is any more legitimate than any other. Today we have adoptive families, multi-racial families, blended families, co-custody families, conditionally separated families, extended families, foster families, gay or lesbian families, and single-parent families, and we are constantly admonished that all viewpoints are equally valid, and all these types of families are equally valid. The really interesting stuff begins when you point out that logically, if *all* definitions of family are equally valid, *then the traditional nuclear family is equally valid!*

You see, that's the problem with people who insist that they are the open-minded, compassionate ones, and yet maintain a strict policy of bullying and intimidating people who don't agree with them into behaving as if they do. (Bullying people into behaving as if they agree with you, by the way, is my personal definition of political correctness, which, having already established that *all* viewpoints are equally valid, is a perfectly valid way of looking at the subject.) In reality, their bottom line often turns out to be "All viewpoints are equally valid.... *except yours!*"

Instead of preaching to you about the importance of families, I'm going to give you a little assignment. Find out which countries on this planet have governmental and ideological systems in which the family has been taken out of the equation. If I were to tell you the names of these countries, that would be leading you to the information I want you to know, and you'd be that much less likely to believe me, so I'm not going to do that. I'd much rather you find out on your own. Some of these countries no longer exist, but some of them still do. Some of them may have changed their names, but they're still here. Then after you've identified them, come back and tell me if any of *those* are countries in which you would like to live.

Unless you are a strict adherent to the ideology of Marxism, in which the institutions of marriage and family officially do not exist, I think we can all agree that any type of family is preferable to no family at all. So if the traditional nuclear family is no more, *and no less* legitimate than any other arrangement, then why should it be preferred over any other type of family? Well, there is been a great deal of research put into answering that question. I took the following examples from a study produced by sociologist Christina Sim entitled Why Families Matter. You can find it on the North Carolina Family Policy Council website. Here are just a few of the conclusions at which the research has arrived. (Keep in mind that although it is not stipulated in *each* example, *traditional nuclear families* and *parental* marriage are the type of family and type of marriage being referred to here.)

- On average, married couples build more wealth than similar singles or cohabiting couples.
- Marriage increases the earning power of men by around 15%.
- Marriage increases life expectancy, even after controlling for race, income and family background.
- Married mothers are half as likely to be victims of domestic violence.
- Across every race and ethnic group, children living in married households have the lowest poverty rates.
- The majority of children who grow up outside of intact families experience at least one year of dire poverty, with family incomes less than half the official poverty threshold.
- Children raised by both biological parents are less likely to experience health problems, less likely to have behavioral or psychological problems, and more likely to graduate from high school.
- Parental divorce reduces a child's life expectancy by four years.
- Parental marriage is associated with a sharply lower risk of infant mortality. On average, having an unmarried mother results in a 50% increase in the risk of infant mortality.
- Compared with peers from intact families, teens whose parents have divorced are 1.5 times more likely to use illicit drugs by age 14.
- Growing up outside of an intact family also increases the likelihood the children will themselves divorce and become unwed parents. For instance, daughters raised outside of intact marriages are approximately three times more likely to end up young, unwed mothers.
- The presence of a father is a significant protective factor in reducing sexual activity and pregnancy among adolescent girls.
- Effective fathering increases the child's chances of developing a positive body image, self-esteem, moral strength, and intellectual and social competence.
- A study of children of divorce showed that father-absent boys had greater learning deficits than those with an involved father
- Marriage creates economically stable units able to contribute more in taxes, and also reduce the likelihood that the state will

have to intervene through expensive crime control and social services programs.

- Teen child bearing costs the US government nearly $7 billion a year.
- Nearly three quarters of government means-tested welfare aid to children goes to single-parent families.
- Over 80% of long term child poverty occurs in broken or never married families.
- On average, marriage reduces the odds that a mother and a child will live in poverty by more than 70%.

Here are a few more pieces of evidence of the value of the traditional family:

- Girls whose parents are divorced face a significantly higher risk of sexual assault, whether they live with their mother or father, according to research by Robin Wilson, a family law professor at Washington and Lee University.
- Children living in step-families or with single parents are at higher risk of physical or sexual assault than children living with both parents, according to several studies co-authored by David Finkelhor, Director of the University of New Hampshire's Crimes Against Children Research Center.

And here is perhaps the most chilling statistic I've ever come across:

- Children living in a household with unrelated adults are nearly *50 times* more likely to *die* of inflicted injuries than children living with two biological parents, according to a study of Missouri data published in the Journal of the American Academy of Pediatrics in 2005.

These are the facts. I didn't make them up, I'm just bringing them to light. This is what the proponents of traditional marriages are standing for, and it's not built on hate, or bigotry, or prejudice. It's built on a strong desire to preserve something, which has been the cornerstone of civilization for thousands of years. It's built on a desire to preserve something, which has been *proven* to be *the best way* to produce happy, prosperous children living in a happy, prosperous society.

But you know, it *is* always **easier** to demonize your opponents than to listen to them and actually learn the truth about their point of view.

Now, all that having been said, riddle me this:

Now that gay marriage has become the law of the land, how many fewer traditional marriages will there be? How many brides and grooms, upon hearing the news have walked out of the church or back yard or City Hall, leaving their future spouses jilted at the altar because their impending marriages no longer mean anything? How many young women planning the perfect wedding have burned their catalogs and scrapbooks because their future marriages have been taken away from them? How many young men, dreaming of a home and a family like the one in which they grew up have denounced those dreams because the institution of the Family has been destroyed? I submit to you now that the number is somewhere around…. zero. Instituting gay marriage does not eliminate one single traditional marriage. Banning gay marriage does not produce a single one more.

The argument against gay marriage is that it will destroy the institution of the family, but tell me this: How will it destroy *your* family? How will gay marriage break up *your* marriage? How does two people entering into a legally recognized relationship 1000 miles away damage *your* relationship? The *institution* of marriage is made up of millions of individual marriages. You and I could examine each and every one of those marriages and when we're done, you could not show me how any single one of them has been damaged in the least, and yet you will insist that they *all* have been damaged by what people who have no connection with them whatsoever have been allowed to do. Is that *really* the argument you want to go with? I invite anyone to explain to me how that works. Tell me how you can protect an institution by excluding from it the people who believe in it and want to honor it the most, while saying nothing about the millions of men and women whose appalling behavior has dishonored and destroyed their own traditional marriages?

As far as I can tell, the argument against gay marriage is based on the logic that if someone were to give the person sitting next to me on the bus a dollar, then the dollar in my pocket would suddenly vanish. It's based on the logic that if someone were to give my neighbor a car, then *my* car would suddenly no longer transport me to work and school and to the grocery store. It's based on the logic that if someone were go give my neighbor a guitar, that my guitar would suddenly no longer make any sound; that I would strum the strings, and no sound would come out.

Now that we have gay marriage, traditional marriage will mean the same thing it has always meant, and always will. To extend the musical metaphor (just for fun), Yoko Ono calling what she calls "music" music, does not magically transform Loreena McKinnett's voice into a cacophonous caterwauling.

I believe in families, and like I said, *any* family is better than no family at all, but some of them not by much. I believe *most* in the type a family that has, for thousands of years, *best* proven to produce the best outcomes for everyone involved. I'm not for a single second suggesting that the proponents of traditional marriage don't have anything to bark about. They're just barking up the wrong tree.

If you really want to point to something that destroys individual families *and* the institution of the Family as a whole, how about something that teaches young men that they can create children and then walk away and abandon them without a second thought, and that they never really have to grow up and accept responsibility for their actions if they don't want to? How about something that teaches young girls that there can actually be financial profit in becoming unwed mothers, and the more times they do it, the more profit there can be? How about something that teaches people that women don't need to marry the fathers of their children; that they can simply substitute what is basically the same relationship; basically *marry the state,* and it will provide everything the fathers of their children would have?

Now where, oh where, are we going to find an institution like *that*?

Author's Note

I have a question to ask you. It is an honest and sincere question and I mean absolutely no disrespect to anyone by asking it. Here goes:

Are you a prude? It's okay if you are, really. Prudes need love too. Honestly, some of my best friends are prudes....

...But if you are, you might want to seriously consider skipping the next two chapters. I'm confident your reading experience with the remaining chapters will still be completely worthwhile. In fact, there are three more completely G-rated chapters after these.

In the next two chapters, I have made no effort to be gratuitously prurient or vulgar.... but neither do I walk on any eggshells. I speak frankly about something without which there would be no life on Earth higher than bacteria and a few insects and lizards...sex.

You know, you can always read them alone when no one else is around, and you can even deny it later. No one ever has to know.

Sexual Orientation

Have you ever noticed how quiet light switches are these days? If you haven't, then you don't remember how they were when I was a kid. They were horrible. Flipping them made little fingers hurt and they made a snapping sound so loud it made your neighbor's cat jump. There was no way you could ever turn on the light without alerting everyone in the house, which made them the bane of a generation of teenagers. They were in a word, *harsh.* It amazes me that anyone could think of anything as fluid, and intangible as human sexuality and sexual orientation in particular, in terms that harsh and absolute, but we do.

Here's a trivia question. How long have homosexuals been around? No, it's not a trick question, well not *completely.* The answer is: a little over 140 years. The term "homosexual" was invented in 1869, and even then, it was an adjective, not a noun. Before then, there was no such thing as "a homosexual." If you could travel back in time 500 years, explain to someone what homosexuality is and then ask them whether or not *they* are a homosexual, their answer might have been something like: "Well…umm… I guess I *am* when I'm with someone of the same sex, and I guess I'm not when I'm with someone of the opposite sex. It's only in the brief little glimpse of human history that is our modern Western culture that what you do between the sheets and with whom constitutes who you are.

In my lifetime, the way society views sexual orientation has gone through some changes that are either interesting, or hilarious depending on how you look at them. For a long time, sexuality was viewed like those light switches, with only two positions. You were either straight or "SNAP" you were *gay.* Those were the only two choices. You either like your own sex and had no interest in the other, or you liked the other and had no interest your own. One was universally good, the other universally evil, perverted, deviant, disgusting, unnatural, immoral and/or communist, take your pick.

There is still plenty of people who feel that way, but somewhere along the way, well into my adult life, the concept of bisexuality entered mainstream thought and reluctantly the switch became a toggle with a position the middle, but strangely, *only for women.* Now, women could either be straight, "SNAP" bisexual, or "SNAP" gay. Now, you can either like women and have no interest in men, like men and have no interest in women, or like them equally. One is still universally good, and for a large segment of the population, the other two are still universally evil, perverted, deviant, etc. For a growing percentage of people though, not only is bisexuality (for women) okay, it can even be trendy. These days, it is not only cute for women to be bisexual, but it's cool for men to dig bisexual women. This was the whole premise behind the short-lived 1992 sitcom Men Behaving Badly, which centered on two single men living next door to two single women. The girls told the guys they were lesbians because they thought it would get them to leave them alone, only to find out it had the opposite effect. It was also one of the major themes in the movie American Pie II, in which a group of male high school graduates, on their own for the summer became obsessed with a couple of women they mistakenly believed to be lesbians. (Just to clarify things a little, it *is* actually *bisexual* women that men dig, not lesbians. Any women we find attractive, but we know will never, *ever* return the favor are going to frustrate and intimidate us, not arouse us.)

I can't tell you how prevalent this notion is, but it's out there, and it's a natural phenomenon. I'm not making it up and you can't make it go away, but if it's any comfort or consolation, you can ignore it. There is no committee somewhere racking their brains like fashion designers in Paris to come up with new sexual perversions. Arbitrary decisions about hemlines may catch on, but sexual arousal doesn't respond to consensus. I suspect it's simply another case of things that always were failing to be suppressed any longer. I think Paul Reiser put it best in the television show Mad About You. When asked by his wife "Why do you guys like that *so much?*" He unhesitatingly replied "It's naked, it's fun and I agree with both of them."

As for men, if popular culture is to be taken at face value, there are still only two positions on the sexual orientation switch. Either you're straight or "SNAP" you're GAY! And by GAY, I mean you've had as little as a single sexual thought about another man at any point in your entire life. If you're a happily married man, but you got drunk on a business trip and had sex with another man, YOU'RE GAY! If you enjoy sex mostly with women, but occasionally with a man, YOU'RE GAY! If you had sex with a man one time twenty years ago, and have had sex exclusively with women ever since, doesn't matter, YOU'RE STILL GAY!

A Perfect example of this mindset is the movie Brokeback Mountain. It's based on a short story from a collection entitled Close Range by Annie Proulx, one of the most phenomenal writers I've ever read. I read the book long before the movie came out, and if I had to sum up the short story Brokeback Mountain in one word, it would be "haunting." (If you *haven't* read the story or seen the movie, just hold your tongue, because you, my friend, do not know what you're talking about.) If you *have* seen the movie or read the story, then you know that both of the main characters have far more relationships and far more sex with the women in their lives than they ever have with each other, and yet Brokeback Mountain will forever be known as "The Gay Cowboy Movie."

Funny thing is, it turns out human beings are not light switches. They're not even three-way light bulbs. If you really want a good electrical metaphor, it would be a rheostat, or a radio dial. On one end, there is complete and uncompromising heterosexuality. On the other is complete and uncompromising homosexuality, but between the two are infinite degrees of difference. There is that person who had a homosexual thought one time and never again. There is the person who has them regularly. (As a matter fact, same sex encounters are the third most common sexual fantasy for heterosexuals of both sexes, *and* opposite sex encounters are the third most common sexual fantasies for homosexuals of both sexes, did you know that?) There is the person who is tempted but will never experiment. There's the person who enjoys a same-sex encounter once in a while, but usually prefers the opposite sex. There are people who are 50/50, 60/40, 75/25, 82/18, or any other ratio mathematically possible. There are even people whose ratio is 0/0 and they don't want to have sex with anyone.

So why have you never heard of any of these people before? Because the vast majority of people don't feel compelled to make their sexual orientation a public issue, and the vocal minority who do, actually want to make *other people's sexuality* a public issue, an idea which only seems more absurd to me the longer I think about it.

Of course they have good reason, don't they? After all, we can't have people running around engaging in *deviant* behavior, can we? Where will it end? They're *abnormal,* you have to worry about them hitting on you when you're out in public, they're always trying to recruit your children into their lifestyle, and it just goes against the natural order of things! Whoa there, big fella! Let's slow down and take these one at a time.

As far as the word "deviant" goes, I'd like to introduce you to a quaint little statistical tool known as the Bell Curve, and it's annoying sidekick, the Standard Deviation. They are ubiquitous. No matter what you're studying, they're going to be there. Any person at any percentile on the Bell Curve (and that means *everyone*) *deviates* from any other person on it by some degree. It's what makes us individuals. If you really want to throw out of the science of statistics, go ahead, but you're going to find it awfully hard to get a lot of things done.

And as for homosexuals who are sick and tired of being thought of as abnormal, I have some unpleasant truth for you too. You *are* abnormal. If something is normal, that means *it is the norm*; the way the *majority* is. For homosexuality to be normal, *heterosexuality* would by definition be *abnormal,* and any species that produces only through abnormal sexual behavior is going to go extinct. *Being abnormal is not automatically bad.* Left-handed people are abnormal. So are redheads, and people with musical talent, and published authors for that matter. I'm sure you could find some way in which every single one of us *deviates from the norm* in some way. Listen, I didn't invent the English language, I'm just using it correctly.

You'll have to bear with me here as I address people who are convinced that homosexuals must recruit their children into their lifestyle "because they can't reproduce, so they have no other way to increase their numbers." I'll try to put this as simply as I can: Gay people are of a different *sexual orientation*, not a different *species*. *Species* have to reproduce to survive, and most of them have done a very poor job of it; 99% of all of them that have ever lived on this planet are extinct. Homosexuals have no compelling interest in increasing their numbers. All they have to do is find each other, and they're pretty good at doing that.

If you're a straight person and you really worry about gay people hitting on you, don't. They want someone who will reciprocate their feelings, and that's not you, now is it? The only place you really have to worry about being accosted by a homosexual is in prison. Stay out of prison, and you'll be okay. Trust me on this.

Lastly, there have *always* been a certain number of homosexuals among us, and there is no indication that there won't always be. I hate to have to break this to you, but having a certain percentage of homosexuals in the human population *is* the natural order of things. Being abnormal and being natural are not mutually exclusive.

Is homosexuality a choice? That's always been the biggy, hasn't it? Is it a choice, and can it be cured? On the one side of the argument, gay people ask the question: Who would ever *choose* this? Who would *choose* a lifestyle in which you are discriminated against, ridiculed, looked down upon, beaten up and sometimes killed? Maybe people who don't believe another person's bedroom activities merit any of those ludicrous overreactions, perhaps? To be perfectly honest, I don't spend a whole lot of time worrying about *other people's* sex lives. I mainly try to concentrate on my own. I have no idea whether or not gay people choose to be gay, but what if they do? It's *their* choice about *their* life, and has no bearing on mine whatsoever. I did not *choose* to be straight, but that doesn't disprove that someone else might have.

When asking whether or not homosexuality is a choice, we tend to fall back on the old habit of thinking of it as a light switch. We restrict ourselves to those two positions. I'll politely remind you again that people are not light switches, and actually, conclusively *proving* anything is a far more rare act than anyone realizes.

I'd like to see anyone conclusively prove or disapprove the following possibilities: For some people, their sexual orientation is a choice, for others it is not. Of those for whom it is, some are happy with their sexuality and some are not. Of those who are unhappy with it, some can be cured, some cannot. Of those who *are* happy, why should they want to be cured?

Even more possibilities open up if you stop viewing sexual orientation as a line between two points. That's a two dimensional figure, and we live in a three-dimensional world. Who is to say that male and female are the only kinds of sexual orientation we can have? Could not some people be *oriented* toward monogamy, while others are *oriented* toward multiple partners? Could not some people be oriented toward private sex, and others toward sex in the presence of others? Could not some be *oriented* toward sadomasochism, or bondage and discipline? Could not some people be oriented toward using sex toys, while others would never dream of touching them?

Some people will say: "Well, those are just personal quirks or tastes. They're just things that some people enjoy, but being straight or gay, now *that's* something we have to formulate public policy around, and control at a societal level!"

That's really where they tip their hand, isn't it? When you get down to the nitty-gritty, the whole ruckus about sexual orientation is really about people trying to control other people's behavior, not because it affects *them* in any way, but because it goes against their notions of how things ought to be. In other words, it's the dreaded "P word" rearing its ugly head again.

It could all be so simple. Just ask these questions: Does the person I'm with like me, respect me, value me as a person and a companion, and desire me? Is the feeling mutual?

We're good!

Pornography

(Don't Let Your Kids Read This Chapter!)

I'm about to tell you a tale of horror and degradation, straight from the pits of Hell. You may want to think twice about reading it, because according to some people, it has the potential to warp your mind, and set you on a path to depravity from which you may never recover. Proceed past this point at your own risk.

A young couple, let's call them Sue and Doug, have just purchased a new renter's insurance policy, and their agent advised them to catalog as many of their valuables as they can. He suggested using their video camera as being the easiest and quickest way to do it. They simply hold up each item in front of the camera, turn it at several different angles and say a few words about it and how much it cost. They've gone through the living room and kitchen, and they're now starting into the bedroom. Halfway through the room, their aging videotape camera goes on the fritz. It looks like they waited just one day too long to upgrade to a digital camera. They spend a few minutes fiddling with it trying to make it work, but having no luck, they set it down on the dresser and go out to get some dinner, not realizing that they haven't actually turned the camera off, and that it just happens to be pointed toward the bed.

Later that evening, they get ready for bed with the camera still sitting on the dresser, still not working. Shortly after they go to bed, Sue starts feeling a little frisky. She rolls over and starts nibbling on Doug's ear until he wakes up. This is not the first time Sue has done this, and Doug knows what's on her mind. Before you know it, nature has taken its course. I'm not going into any details; you're just going to have to use your imagination. It's just two married people, making love in the privacy of their own

197

bedroom, completely unaware of the horror that is about to befall one of them.

Silently, and without warning, the short circuit in their video camera becomes intermittent, and the camera starts recording. Oh my God! Suddenly, what was a few seconds ago a wholesome scene of love and affection is now ruined for all time. One second ago, Sue was making love to her husband, but in the blink of an eye she is being horribly *degraded*. How can she ever recover from this? How will she ever show her face in public? Can anything ever be right with the world again?

But wait. Just a suddenly, the video camera shorts out again and stops working, saving Sue from a fate worse than death. The sanctity of their marital relationship is restored and everything is okay again. The nightmare appears to be over.

But is it? Cruelly, the video camera starts recording again. Poor, poor Sue. Once again, she's been dehumanized and degraded, her dignity and humanity destroyed, reduced to nothing more than a piece of meat, and the worst thing is, she doesn't even know it.

Then, the camera goes off again, and everything is okay. It comes on again, and she is being degraded. Off-again, okay. On again, horrible degradation! Off, respect and love. On, degradation! Oh someone make it stop! Stop reading! Look away! Look away now!

What's that? What about Doug, you ask? Oh, he was just fine. Nothing happened to him.

The loudest argument I hear against pornography is that it degrades women. I'll wager that the vast majority of the people who present this argument have never in their lives seen a single second of pornography. Someone is going to have to explain to me how two people having sex is okay, but a *visual depiction* of two people having sex is intrinsically degrading to one of them, and not the other. If that is the case, then why is the woman *not* being degraded if the same two people have sex in the absence of a video camera? (Actually, there are people who will tell you that she is, but that's another discussion.)

Is it because in pornography, women are portrayed as enjoying and even seeking out sex? Well, we can't have any of *that,* now can we? I mean, if women start enjoying sex on a regular basis, where will it end? If that's the case, wasn't Sue degrading *herself* when she *initiated* sex with Doug? And again, if the enjoyment of sex is degrading, then why are men not degraded by being portrayed as enjoying it?

Consider this. People in ancient Polynesia believed that the earth was made fertile by the sexual coupling of their gods, and that the gods were aroused by the coupling of men and women. Sex was a regular component of their religious ceremonies. There are Hindu temples in India, a country in which people are not allowed to kiss in movies (They substitute rolling around on the ground while holding each other, I kid you not) which are literally covered with unequivocal depictions of men and women engaged in sexual acts, literally carved into the stone of the structures. You can find the same images carved into the frescos of private homes in the ruins of Pompeii. Now, when the Polynesians were practicing their religion, and the Hindus were designing and building their temples, did they actually contemplate how to honor their deities and then say, "Hey, I know, let's degrade women!" Or, is it possible that they considered sex a life-affirming act of spirituality, worthy of being depicted for all to see? Could it be even remotely possible that it *is*, and that our society has just conditioned us to reject that way of thinking? People say they don't like pornography because it's degrading to women? Is it possible that they say it's degrading to women because they don't like it?

Another big argument against pornography is that it is highly addictive and warps the minds of those who view it. The theory is that if you consume something less than actual pornography, say, the Sports Illustrated Swimsuit Issue for example, you will be excited and aroused, but it won't last for long. You'll become desensitized to it, and it won't have the desired affect. Soon, you will be compelled to seek out something stronger, like Playboy Magazine. *That* will work for a while; it will get you excited and aroused, but it won't last long. Soon you'll be graduating to hard-core pornography magazines, where you will find images of actual sex acts. Soon though, even they will fail to give the effect you desire and increasingly can't do without. You'll have to start viewing pornographic videos, and when those don't work anymore, you'll have to find S&M and bondage videos, and finally snuff films. Where do you go from there? It's obvious isn't it? You'll have to start having actual sex; immoral, predatory, woman-degrading sex. Where will it end? It will end with you raping and murdering women and dumping their bodies in dumpsters and roadside ditches. It all started with the Sports Illustrated Swimsuit Issue, and once the process was set in motion, there was nothing you or anyone else could do to stop it. The outcome was inevitable. That's the dark, satanic mind control power of pornography.

This argument actually has its basis in fact, and then it just goes completely insane. Again, it's the phenomenon of habituation. Whenever a living thing is repeatedly exposed to a stimulus, its reaction to that stimulus diminishes over time. It happens with any kind of stimulus; food, music, perfume, movies, anything we are exposed to over and over again, and it happens with every living thing from flatworms on up to human beings.

Here's my question. If we are compelled to continually seek out more and more intense stimuli, as the anti-pornography argument maintains, then why are we not compelled to eat more and more intensely flavored foods, until we end up pouring acid on our tongues in a desperate effort to excite our hopelessly desensitized taste buds? Why are we not compelled to listen to louder and more cacophonous music, until we end up plunging ice picks into our eardrums because nothing we can listen to will stimulate them? Oh, I forgot…. it's because this is *pornography* were talking about, with the dark satanic mind control power!

There are some people who actually believe that. I don't. I don't believe it because I believe the vast majority of people are reasonable. If their favorite song no longer sends shivers up their spine, they'll put something else on for a while. Pretty soon, they'll feel like listening to it again. If they get tired of eating pizza, they'll eat something else. Sooner or later, (usually *sooner* for me) their craving for pizza will return....and, if whatever type of erotica they enjoy ceases to arouse them, they'll put it down and do something else for a while.

Are there people who become addicted to pornography? Of course there are. There are also people who become addicted to alcohol, and tobacco, and illicit drugs, and collecting trash, and dressing up as furry animals, and eating couch cushions, but I don't see a whole lot of people morally outraged by any of *those things.* Have you ever noticed that there's no moral taboo against poking yourself in the eye with a sharp stick? Do you know why? It's because nobody *wants* to do *that*! People say they don't like pornography because it's addictive. Is it possible they say it's addictive because they don't like it?

If you're getting the impression by now that I'm some sort of cheerleader for pornography, you're wrong. I'm not. I'd be lying if I told you I have never seen any. Unlike 99% of the people who rail against it, I have, and as someone who's actually seen pornography, I can speak with at least a modicum of authority when I tell you this: *99% of all pornography is pure crap*, and I have better things to do than try to find the other 1%.

It's crap because it's fake. People look at pornography for the first time expecting to see sex. Instead, they see people going through the motions of sex for money, and that fact is glaringly obvious (at least it is 99% of the time.) Now, I suppose if you really do view sex as nothing more than the process of inserting one body part into another and creating friction, then I guess pornography could fit the definition. If that's truly all you consider sex to be, I feel sorry for you, but I can't fix you, and it wouldn't be my job to fix you if I could. For those of us who are more highly evolved as human beings, sex is a whole heck of a lot more.

Let me ask you this: If you've gone to a concert in the last twenty years, then you know how expensive concert tickets have become. Would you pay that kind of money to watch someone stand on a stage for two hours and play *air guitar?* That's exactly what you get when you watch pornography.

There are plenty of other reasons why, if pornography suddenly vanished off the face of the earth, the quality of *my* life would not be diminished one iota. (By the way, I wouldn't hold my breath waiting for that to happen if I were you. The only way you could be certain you had accomplished it would be to confiscate every video camera and smartphone on earth, and even then, I guarantee you *someone* out there would go dig that Super 8 camera out of that box in the attic and go to town.)

So, without further ado, here it is, from the home office in Toledo Ohio, My *Top 10 List of Reasons Why Pornography Really Isn't Worth Your Time.* (I must caution you again, if you think you'll be offended by descriptions of the production values that go into the making of a pornographic video, stop reading now. If you've never seen any pornography, you would just be confused anyway. For those of you who think you can handle it and have a vivid enough imagination, you might be able to take it as tongue-in-cheek as I intend it to be.)

Reason Number 10: *What's with the shoes?* I'll wager that 99.9% of all women on earth do *not* have sex while wearing 5 inch, chrome, platform shoes with 9-inch stiletto heals, so why the heck does it seem like 99% of all women in porn videos do? "Well, we have to keep the people with shoe fetishes happy", the porn producers will say. Why? Why do the shoe fetishists rate so highly? What about the people with fetishes for coveralls, or cardboard boxes, or lime Jell-O? You don't see *those* in every damn porn flick you watch! Most people don't even know what a fetish really is, anyway. I once made the mistake of telling one of my wife's coworkers that I really liked the way a certain pair of her shoes (my wife's that is, not her coworker's), look on her. Her instant and irritatingly predictable response was "Oh, so you have a shoe fetish!" No, I don't. *I just like the way her shoes look on her.* An actual fetish is a specific psychological process. If I had a true shoe fetish, it would progress through three stages: Stage 1: I get turned on when she wears the shoes. Stage 2: I *can't* get turned on *unless* she wears the shoes. Stage 3: I don't even need her anymore; all I need is the shoes. Where is the fun in that?

If I wanted to see any kind of footwear on a woman during sex, it would probably be something that shows me she likes being energetic and physical, so if any kind of shoe is going to turn me on, it would be a pair of Nike running shoes, maybe with a pair of those cute little ankle socks....uh, let's move on.

Reason Number Nine: *Can we have just a little bit of plot, please!* Scene: interior, nighttime. A young man is standing in front of an elevator. The door opens and a young blond woman steps out. Cut to them doing it.

Excuse me? Did I miss a few minutes here? Did I fall asleep? Every Action Adventure movie needs a few good explosions and car chases, but would you watch an entire Action Adventure movie that was *nothing but* two hours of explosions and car chases? (I saw one that came close once. It was a Robert DeNiro film called Ronin, and it was possibly one of the most boring movies I ever sat through.) That's the way pornography is made. No character development, no plot, just sex. Again for those of you for whom sex is nothing more than the physical act, that may be enough. For the rest of us, it's sadly lacking.

It's been said that if men like it, it's pornography; if women like it, it's *erotica*. I've heard more than one woman say that if pornography depicted an actual relationship between a man and a woman; an actual emotional connection between them before they started to have sex, it would go a long way toward making it worth their while to take a look at it. That's not to say that there are no women who enjoy pornography as it is, because as much as you might not like hearing it, there are.

Will Pornography ever change in this respect? Will it ever start incorporating some of the things that make mainstream movies worth watching? Believe it or not, there are some makers of erotica out there who try to do just that. (Some of them are even *women!*) They are the other 1%, but it's a whole lot easier to make money doing it the way it's always been done, and making money is mostly what it's all about.

Reason Number Eight: *Where did you find these people?* If you want me to watch your dirty movie, don't show me muscle-bound bodybuilders and prostitutes. That's what most of the people in porn films look like, and that's how they act. Why? Are you seriously suggesting that *these* are the only kind of people who have sex? Are you suggesting that *these* are the only kind of people have *good* sex? How stupid do you think we are? If you really want to turn me on, don't show me body builders and hookers; show me *real people!* Show me the guys I work with (Well okay, don't show me the obese ones, and while we're at it, I don't want to see them dancing in country music videos either.) Show me soccer moms with crow's feet and pooches. Yes people, I know you don't want to hear it, but we have to face the fact; *moms have sex.* It's true, they do. Yes*, they do.* YES, THEY DO! Oh for crying out loud, how do you think they got to *be* moms in the first place?

Reason Number Seven: *To make a film worth watching, you need ACTORS!* One thing you will not see in any pornographic video is any real passion. Of course, that's because there isn't any, but if the people in these videos could act their way out of a wet paper bag, they could at least create the *illusion* of passion. Jimmy Stewart was never actually a cowboy in the Old West, but when you saw him in Cheyenne Autumn or How the West Was Won, he made you believe he was, because man, *that guy could act!* That's one thing about pornography that will never change. The people who can act don't appear in porn films, and the people in porn films can't act. Am I expecting too much from the producers of porn? No I'm not. I don't *expect* anything from them, hence my not holding my breath waiting for it to happen.

While we're on the subject of acting, we have to talk about the sounds. I'm sure some people have sex in absolute silence. Others make a lot of noise, but I honestly don't believe that *anyone* makes the *exact same noise* over and over again hundreds of times over the course of twenty minutes. (Some of them *do* say the same *word* over and over again for 20 minutes. I found that out once in a hotel with very thin walls, when I really would rather have gotten some sleep. I'm glad my wife and son weren't with me that night.) Short of actually recording one moan and looping it over and over again, I don't see how they do it. A couple of minutes of that, and it is no longer arousing, it's like fingernails on a chalkboard.

Reason Number Six: *People are not pretzels.* Real people have sex lying in beds, occasionally lying on couches, or lying in the back seats of cars. Real people have sex on *all* their hands and knees, sitting and maybe even standing. What real people do *not* do is have sex with their bodies contorted into positions that olympic gymnasts could not comfortably hold for more than a minute. It seems to me that when most of your concentration is required just to maintain a pose, there's not going to be that much left over for enjoyment of physical sensations. I don't think any of these positions are even in the Kama Sutra. Of course, I've never actually *read* the Kama Sutra. Maybe I should.

Reason Number Five: *Location, Location, Location!* Maybe I'm wrong about this, but I've always assumed one of the things these movies are supposed to do is let you put yourself in the characters place; to let you experience vicariously what they are experiencing on the screen. I've had dreams where I found myself in my underwear on a public street. *I was not enjoying myself!* So if you expect me to relate to people doing it in a department store, forget it! I know there are people who are turned on by public sex, but I would think that if you want to make the *most* money, you would produce a product that the *most* people could relate to. These people really need a Business 101 class.

Reason Number Four: *Your technique is all wrong!* Come on, people. If you've had sex a few dozen times, you know what works and what doesn't. You know what feels good, and what these people are doing ain't it. It looks like they're doing it not with the intent of giving pleasure to their partner, but giving the best view to the camera.... oh wait, that's right, *they are!* I'm glad these things aren't intended to be instructional videos, because if we *all* tried to have sex like this, it would be so un-stimulating and un-inspiring, no one would want to do it, and the human race would just go extinct.

Reason Number Three. (Yawn!) *Can we move this along a little please?* I tried to do a little bit of research into how long the average sex act lasts. I can't get a straight answer. Every entry I found on the Internet says things like "Well, it's different for different people" and "It can last anywhere from 10 to 30 minutes." These people are obviously a little fuzzy on the definition of the word "average." It's one number, pure and simple! Just give it to me! Where's Alfred Kinsey when you need him? Anyhow, take any number you like, whether it's 10 minutes or 45, and you'll probably find it's still only half the duration of the average act of oral sex in a porn film, and if the woman giving it seems every bit as enthusiastic toward the end of it as she does at the beginning (which isn't much), I can understand why. Again, if you're trying to produce the illusion of real sex, you're way off the mark. I once heard a comedienne put it this way: "Can we keep this to 15 minutes? 'Cause Mama's got shit to do."

Reason Number Two: *Body parts don't have sex, people have sex.* If you go to the Louvre, you will find sculptures of nude men and women. You will find paintings of nude men and women. You will even find paintings of nude men and women in erotic situations, even if they are merely suggested or alluded to. All of these are accepted as serious art. If you care to look for it, you can find Chinese and Hindu erotic art that is not suggested or alluded to, but leaves absolutely nothing to the imagination. Again, these are accepted within these cultures as legitimate artistic expression. What you will *not* find in any of these places are portrayals of human body parts, by themselves, engaged in sex acts. So why is it that in every porn film you see close-ups of people's genitalia going at it like the pistons of a car engine for minutes on end? If you insist on saying that pornography is dehumanizing, I'd say *this* is about as close as it gets, for *both* partners.

And now, the **Number One Reason** pornography is a waste of your time......*No matter how it begins, you end up watching men masturbate!* If you don't get this one, I'm sorry, but you're on your own. You're just going to have to watch a dirty movie and find out for yourself.

I would be remiss if I ended this chapter without addressing the subject of pornography and children. You will hear opponents of pornography say that its producers are *targeting* your children. That is nonsense. The producers of pornography have one objective, and one objective only, and that is to *make money.* Your kids don't have any. They may be profiteers, but they're not stupid.

It is true that with just a few clicks, your kids could be watching pornography right on your home computer, if they know the specific clicks to make. I wish it weren't, but it is. Fortunately, it's easy to put a filter on your Internet access so they won't be able to do this. I think an infinitely preferable situation would be to build a relationship with your kids in which they are trustworthy, and they will not go looking for it if you tell them not to. Then, put a filter on your computer anyway.

Do I think it's okay for kids to be exposed to pornography? I absolutely, categorically do not. Pornography should have absolutely no part in shaping kids' concepts, ideas or opinions about sex. That's *your* job as a parent. You can shirk that responsibility if you want, but the job's going to get done, sometime, by someone. It's best if it's you, so man up.

And I am contradicting myself here? If I really think there's nothing inherently *evil* about pornography, then why do I think kids should be protected from it? Well, I also think kids should be protected from guns, sharp knives, alcohol, live electrical wires, and automobiles, even though I don't think any of those things are inherently evil either.

I'd like to come full circle here and come back to the idea that pornography is degrading to women. Have you watched any mainstream television lately? Have you noticed how it treats men? It is truly disturbing how often fathers in particular are portrayed as bumbling imbeciles. The epitome of this trend had to be the America On Line commercial in which a young boy tells you: "It's so easy, even my *dad* can do it." When you become as outraged at the degradation of men and fathers on television as you are about the perceived degradation of women in pornography, I'll be ready to talk.

And while we're talking about television, Animal Planet should have a warning before every wildlife documentary that follows the life cycle of any animal, because they don't seem to mind showing you demonstrations of animal sex that leave nothing, and I mean *nothing* to the imagination. Without even asking you first, they show you full blown, in-your-face animal pornography of horses having sex, gophers having sex, antelopes having sex, rabbits having sex, chimpanzees having sex, otters having sex, rhinoceri having sex, mountain goats having sex, people hav.....NOW WAIT JUST A MINUTE! YOU CAN'T SHOW THAT! THAT'S...**IMMORAL!**

Now what I want to know is, if you take the video of the horses having sex, and *show it to a horse.....*

The Poor

Stereotype: A widely held but fixed and oversimplified image or idea of a particular type of person or thing.

False Dichotomy: A situation in which two opposing viewpoints are presented as the only alternatives, when numerous others are available.

The fact that you can fit all of Humanity into the state of Rhode Island not withstanding, there is one way in which there really are too damn many people in the world. In any group that has seven *billion* members, you will always be able to find people who perfectly fit any stereotype you care to come up with. So when someone puts a post on Facebook intimating that you are more likely to be *hated* if you're gay, or black, or an immigrant, and you reply that "No one hates poor people just because they're poor", and yet another person replies "There are those who do", where are you supposed to go with that? You can't say, "No, they don't, dammit, be reasonable!" because *they're right!* Somewhere out there, there really is someone who hates poor people for no other reason than they don't have any money. There is also someone out there who hates black people just because they're black and another who hates white people just because they're white. There are a few out there who hate *themselves* just because they're white. Somewhere out there, there is a gay person who just can't resist hitting on straight people. Does it make any sense at all? Maybe not, but that's the world we live in.

Here's where *I'm* going with it. Can we agree, for purposes of this discussion to exclude those people who literally *are* walking, breathing stereotypes? Good, let's consider that done.

Stereotyping is a really bad, closed minded, despicable thing to do.... when *other* people do it, right? I mean, *you* would never stereotype anyone, would you? On the other hand, dismantling stereotypes; explaining why they are for the most part completely invalid is a very good and noble thing to do.... when *you* do it, right? All too often, it seems to depend entirely on whether or not you like the person being stereotyped.

I'm going to throw out the name of a group of people, and let's see what is the first thing that comes to your mind. Ready?

Wealthy people.

How many of you thought *good* things?

Now, how many of you thought this: They're selfish and greedy and they hate poor people. They think the poor are where they are because of their own bad choices in life, that they are a burden on society, that they made their own bed, and now they should have to lay in it.

As with all things, there are two possibilities here. Either people wind up where they are because of their own choices and actions, or they don't. Let's do a little deconstruction here and explore the second possibility first. Let's assume that people are *not* responsible for their own outcomes; that they are where they are because of what has been done to them by other people, and the only solution is for other people (and I mean *other* other people, not the ones who have done all these horrible things to them) to help them. Let me ask you this. How is anyone going to help these poor people, if they themselves are just as poor? So, the people doing the helping have to be better off than the people getting the help, right? How did *they* get to be better off? If *they* are not responsible for *their* own situations, then they must've been helped by still *other* people who, not being responsible for *their* own outcomes, must've been helped by still *other* people, who, not being responsible for *their* own outcomes....

You're going to run out of people. Sooner or later you're going to come to that one last person on Earth who has enough wealth to help everyone else. Okay, where did *he* get his wealth? Some people will tell you the answer is simple; he stole it from all the poor people because he was greedy, selfish and powerful. The problem is, *selfish greedy people don't help other people!* So in order to reconcile this theory logically, we either have to have massive numbers of "haves" who *aren't* selfish and greedy and *are* willing to help the "have-nots", **or,** people really are responsible for their own life choices. Actually, there is a third possibility. It could be (gasp).... *both!*

Now onto the opposing theory; that the choices people make influence the outcomes they get. Is there any actual evidence to support this? As it turns out, there *is* evidence.... a lot of it. A lot of research has been put into this over many, many years. I realize that I may have quoted Mark Twain elsewhere in this book saying "There are three kinds of lies; Lies, Damn lies, and Statistics", but the truth of the matter is, if you ask millions upon millions of people the same questions enough times over a sufficient number of years, and you get the same correlations year after year, decade after decade, the likelihood that there is *no* causality involved approaches zero.

As it turns out, there are six actions that correlate very closely to membership in the middle and upper classes in this country. The number of people who did all six of these things and wound up in lifelong poverty is so small, it's not statistically significant. The converse is also true; the number of people who did *not* do these things and *did not* wind up being poor is also too small to be statistically significant. The six things are:

1. Finishing high school.
2. Taking the first job you can get.
3. Immediately starting to work toward getting a better one.
4. Waiting until marriage to start a family.
5. Staying married to raise them.
6. Not committing any crimes.

The evidence supports the hypothesis that if a person accomplishes these six things, their chances of ending up in poverty, and more importantly, their *children's* chances of ending up in poverty are *just about zero*. I didn't make this stuff up off the top of my head. I didn't falsify the responses on the surveys taken over the many, many years, and I didn't hack into all the computers and change the data. *This is the evidence.*

Now I'm going to say something that is going to anger a lot of people. Angering them is not something I set out to do and to be perfectly honest, I'd rather not do it, but I guess I have to show my backbone sooner or later, right? So here goes. Each of these things is, for the vast majority of people, *a choice*. The majority of people are not *forced* out of high school. The majority of people are not *perpetually prevented* from finding a job. Once they get it, the majority of people are not *prohibited* from working toward advancement. The majority of people are not *forced* to have children out of wedlock (birth control is *99% effective!*) The majority of parents are not *forced* to divorce, and with incredibly few exceptions no one is *forced* to break the law. At each juncture, they can either do the things that lead to good outcomes, or they can choose not to. Of course there are going to be exceptions, but if you want to start arguing that any exception invalidates any rule, then you've pretty much invalidated every argument in the world, including your's.

Using the word "choice" is kind of like throwing a switch in front of an oncoming train. It's kind of hard to get 100,000 tons of steel back on the other track after you've thrown it, so I might as well get it over with and say it. The evidence supports the hypothesis that at certain points in people's lives, their choices influence the outcomes they get later in life. If at each of these junctures, they make good choices, they tend to get good results most of the time, and if they make bad choices, they tend to get bad results most of the time. There's another way of putting it, and even though it is supported by the evidence, it will send roughly half the people reading this into fits of rage:

Free people are responsible for their own lives.

Whoa! Did you feel that? Did you feel the ground move just now? It wasn't an earthquake, although I'm pretty sure it would've measured at least 3.5 on the Richter scale. No, that was the Earth actually moving from millions of people reading this (Hopefully. Hey, I can dream, can't I?) simultaneously making the gargantuan leap to the conclusion that just like every other wealthy person in America, *I don't want poor people to be helped.* Well, I have five things to say about that:

1. I never said it.
2. It's not true.
3. How do you get from "People are responsible for their own lives" to "Poor people shouldn't be helped" anyway? Show

me some logical connection between those two statements. There is none.

4. Even if it *were* true, it wouldn't make any sense. Even if wealthy people really did hate poor people because they are a burden on society, *if you don't help them, they will* **continue** *to be a burden on society.* You would be perpetuating the very situation you're railing against. What sense does that make?

5. I currently drive a 21-year-old Ford Ranger pickup with a headliner that's literally falling out on my head and a radio, heater, windshield washer and interior lights that don't work. You call *that wealthy?*

There are actually a couple of problems with the blanket statement "Free people are responsible for their own lives." The biggest is, it's a discussion ender. People on the Left stop listening, because they think anyone saying that has just demonstrated an obvious hatred for the poor, and people on the Right stop talking because they consider it an obvious truth that needs no further explanation. Neither of these is necessarily the truth, the whole truth, and nothing but the truth.

What if I told you that a person might be totally responsible for their own poverty, but cannot he held responsible for improving their own situation? Not making any sense? I'm about to.

Let's consider the captain of an aircraft carrier. (Yeah, I know, just stay with me!) He is responsible for every aspect of the carriers operation. So, here's what we're going to do. We're going to throw him in the brig and hand over the bridge to the most inexperienced Seaman Recruit on the ship. Whatever decisions he makes, whatever commands he gives, and whatever disastrous results ensue, the *Captain* will be held responsible. How do you think that is going to turn out for everyone involved? Here's another good question: *Why is this never done?*

Here is another example a little closer to home. There is a thug somewhere in your city with a rap sheet as long as your arm. On it is everything from arson, to home invasion, to armed robbery to murder. He is a sociopath bordering on psychopath, with no regard for the law and a proven callous disregard for his fellow human being. From now on, *you* are going to be responsible for *his* actions. The next time he commits a crime, the police are coming after you. How do you like *them* apples?

What ties both of these scenarios and the plight of the poor together is this: ***There can be no responsibility without control.*** It is not only possible but far too commonplace for a person to fall into such dire poverty that they no longer have the resources to take control of their own lives. My son has often heard me say, "Okay, so it's not your fault. It really isn't. That doesn't mean you can't do anything about it, and it's sure as hell doesn't mean you shouldn't have to do anything about it." The difference is, *my son has always had the resources he needs to improve his situation.* There are people out there who just plain don't. It is unreasonable to expect a person to "pull themselves up by their own bootstraps" when they literally have no bootstraps to pull on. The homeless veteran standing at an intersection holding up a cardboard sign has no bootstraps. If he did, he wouldn't be there. (Yes, I know there are panhandlers who get into their Audis at the end of the day and drive to their three bedroom homes, but we agreed to leave them out of this discussion, remember?) The 18-year-old kid getting off a bus a thousand miles from the foster home she was thrown out of by her profiteering foster parents a week ago, has no bootstraps. The man being released from prison and literally put on the street in his underwear without a cent to his name (I'm not exaggerating. This actually happened. I know the man personally) has no bootstraps. The battered wife sleeping in her car after her bank account has been cleaned out by her abusive husband because she had the temerity to escape from him, has no bootstraps. The couple sleeping in a shelter with their children, even if they *are* being given a place to sleep and food to eat each day, still have no bootstraps.

At this point, whether these people ended up where they are through their own choices, or by circumstances beyond their control **is irrelevant.** The reality of the here and now is that they don't have the resources to better their lives. They need our help and they should get it. They should get it because they are human beings. They are someone's mothers, daughters, fathers and sons and brothers and sisters. They should get it because they all deserve the opportunity to *earn* the dignity, self respect and *freedom* that come *only* from standing on your own two feet and making your own way in the world. No welfare check, no matter how big, can replace that. They should also get it *so that they will no longer be a burden on society.*

There is another side of the coin when I say there is no responsibility without control. To whatever extent you make a government agency responsible for your life, *that agency is going to control your life.* The people living on public assistance are literally not free to get themselves a better job. If they do, they often risk losing money they still need. People living in public housing are not free to move to a better neighborhood, or another state if they want without risking ending up back on the streets. This is not freedom. Sure, they are provided with shelter, and food, and maybe even a little pocket money…. just like a *prisoner* is provided with shelter, and food and maybe even a little pocket money. It's a very low security prison to be sure, but in some important ways, a prison nonetheless.

Ask anyone living on welfare or in government housing if they have the same freedom I do. Does it really stretch the bounds of credulity so much to imagine that I want poor people to have the same freedom I enjoy? Perhaps, just perhaps, you could consider the possibility that it is not the poor some people hate, but a system that claims to be compassionate; that claims to give them dignity, but in reality ends up keeping them like animals in a stable.

I'm going to go a step further with the idea of helping the poor, and this is going to anger the other half of the people reading this (Hey, I warned you on the cover of the book, so don't get all indignant now.) It is very easy to tell any of these people "Get a job", but how many of us have put a second's thought into what it takes to *keep* a job? First of all, it takes a marketable skill; the knowledge and ability to do something that will add value to an employer's enterprise, and that often means education. It takes a place to live that you won't get thrown out of the minute you start making some money. It takes clothes that are presentable to the management and clientele of that business. It takes transportation to get to that job, whether it is a reliable car, or a bicycle, (Don't laugh. I once spent two years in Boulder Colorado with a bicycle as my *only* means of transportation, year-round, and I loved it!) Or public transportation, or yes, even walking (if you are lucky enough to have two healthy, functional legs.) These four things all have one thing in common. *You can't get them on your own if you don't have a job.*

"So exactly what are you suggesting here?", you say. "Are you suggesting free education, and free clothes and a free car to every poor person in America, for Pete's sake?"

I'm suggesting putting people back on their feet; really, truly putting them solidly back on their own two feet, *and then expecting them to walk.* I'm suggesting giving people the tools to take control of their own destiny, *and then expecting them to take it.* If that entails an education and clothes and access to transportation, then that's what it entails. I didn't say a *really nice* car.

As for it being free? The truth is, nothing is free. If one man is getting something and not paying for it, another man is paying for it and not getting it. Nothing is free. People can be paid back though. They can be paid back by getting to live in a freer, more prosperous society in which they have less of the fruits of their labor confiscated to "help" an endless stream of poor people stretching into eternity."

But you said it yourself", you say. "It's an endless stream of poor people, stretching into eternity. You're talking about an even more massive welfare state that we have now. We can't do it! It would bankrupt the country! There are just too many of them!"

There are too many of them *now*. An endless stream is not inevitable. If we can help only 10% of them, *and they stay on their feet*, then we have 10% fewer people to help and 10% more resources to help the other 90%. If we can help *another* 10%, and they stay helped, then we have *20%* fewer people in need of help, and *20%* more resources available to help the other 80%. The way it's done now, simply giving a handout, forever, with no expectation of any personal responsibility, gives noone any incentive to *stay* on their feet. This is a mistake people with an agenda count on us to keep making. They want us to go on assuming that the future is going to be just as bad if not worse than the present. Can you name any period of time in the last thousand years when technology and human ingenuity did *not* eventually improve the human condition? We have the ability to make things better. The question is: *Do we have the will*?

Do you remember those six actions I mentioned earlier? if you don't, Here they are again:

1. Finishing high school.
2. Taking the first job you can get.
3. Immediately starting to work toward getting a better one.
4. Waiting until marriage to start a family.
5. Staying married to raise them.
6. Not committing any crimes.

Here's a couple of questions for you: How many adults, after being given the opportunity and resources to truly prosper in their own lives and using them, are going to turn around and tell their children to make the same poor choices they made, and wind up where they were? How many children, after watching their parents use those tools and resources to turn their lives around, are going to discount the actions they've seen with their own eyes lead to a better life, and take the ones they've seen lead to poverty? Are there a few of them? Sure, but contrary to what some would have you believe, as a rule people are not stupid.

Can you imagine what this country would be like after a few generations of Americans accomplish all six of these things? We would be left with an exceedingly small minority of people who have fallen on hard times through no fault of their own, and we could help them far more easily and effectively with far more abundant resources. Do you really think the people whom you claim "hate the poor" would have just as much resistance to helping them then?

Getting the next generation of Americans to do these six things is what is going to put an end to the endless stream of the poor, not carrying them through the rest of their lives. I never said it would be easy; I'm saying it's *possible.* I'm saying the people who insist to you that the way we're dealing with it now is the *only* way to do it; that it's the *compassionate* way, the caring way, and if you disagree, then you're part of the problem, are *lying* to you. It will probably be damn hard to reverse a mindset that has been inculcated into the minds of millions of people for seventy years, but if you really, truly care about the plight of the poor, which is the better end result: An endless stream of poor people, needing assistance for all eternity (and getting it), or very small number of temporarily poor people, who could be put back on their feet not by massive bloated government programs, but by the good will of their fellow human beings? That is, if you *really, truly care* about the poor.

In other words, do you want a Band-Aid, or do you want a cure?

One side of this argument seems to be based on the premise that people are stupid and helpless, and they must be taken care of. (Either that, or they are evil and predatory and must be controlled.) I believe the other side is built on the premise that people are smart and capable, and as John Stossel once said "If you leave them alone, they will solve most of their own problems." I'll add that the problems they don't solve today, they will solve tomorrow, because you don't fix today's problems with today's technology or today's thinking. If you could, they wouldn't be today's problems.

I know there are people out there who will never be sold on these ideas. Here's a question for them: Instead of carrying poor people through their lives, I'm talking about putting them exactly where *you* started, with no more and no less of the advantages *you* had or the challenges *you've* overcome. Given that same starting point, the same opportunities and the same resources, why would you imagine that they would *not* succeed just as much as you have? Is there something about them that makes them fundamentally different from you, and renders them incapable of doing that?

One final question; it's a long one: If you truly believe that there will *always* be millions upon millions of poor people, who *despite* being "just as good as the rest of us", will *always* need to be taken care of, generation after generation, because they have been oppressed, or disenfranchised, or exploited....because they're Black, or Hispanic, or LGBT, or tattooed, or have red hair, and can *never* overcome their past....

.... And *I* believe that no matter who they are, or where they came from, or what they've done, that they are perfectly capable, given the same starting point, of taken charge of *their own* lives, making *their own* way in the world, of succeeding just as much and as you and I *and no longer needing our help* **because** they are just as good as the rest of us....

Who really believes *more* in dignity and equality for everyone....

you....or me?

The Hometown Plan

I'd like you to do another thought experiment with me. Here's the situation: The high school basketball teams, both the boys and the girls, need a new backboard for the gym. The reason is, last Friday night, Nancy McFarland hung on the rim after she slam dunked the ball just like she'd seen Michael Jordan do, and it broke the hoop right off along with a good chunk of the backboard. Coach Higgins took a look at it and determined that it couldn't be fixed. Nancy said she feels terrible about breaking the backboard. She shrugged her shoulders and rather sheepishly said it just seemed like a cool idea at the time. Coach Higgins said he wouldn't discipline her, this time, but I think I just saw a little bit of the grin on her face as she walked away and I think a few of her teammates thought it was pretty cool too.

So there's the problem. Now I'd like to propose two solutions. The first solution is this: The ladies in the Lions Club auxiliary can have a bake sale this weekend. The Gazette has already offered to run an ad in the community section free of charge. The ladies auxiliary can give the money they raise to coach Higgins, and he can go over to Dick's Sporting Goods in Shelbyville and order a new backboard and basket. Tom Sweeney over at Dick's says it will take three days to arrive. Coach Higgins can pick it up in his truck and take it over to the high school, where several of the boys from the team, their fathers and a few of the guys from the Lions Club have already volunteered to help put it up.

OK, so that's the first plan. We'll call it plan A, or better yet, the Hometown Plan.

Here's the second option: The basketball teams can get a new backboard through a brand-new Federal Government program. The program was first conceived of four years ago, when a lobbyist for a major sporting goods company (who by the way pulls in a six-figure income) took a congressman who represents a district in another state 2000 miles away from our little town, out to dinner at a fancy Georgetown restaurant that neither you or I could ever afford to patronize, six times, thereby convincing said congressmen that broken basketball backboards are a matter of urgent national concern, worthy of thousands of hours of Congress's time. The bill creating the program, the "Proving We Love Our Children Through Affordable Basketball Goals Act", is 1300 pages long, will generate 242 pages of paperwork for each basketball backboard acquired through it, and contains 159 pages of new federal regulations, because after all, if the Federal Government doesn't regulate basketball goals, anarchy will inevitably ensue (you *know* that, don't you?)

It'll take the high school just 18 short months to acquire the new backboard through this program, but the great thing is, it will be *free!* Well, that is if you don't count the millions of dollars in salaries paid to all those congressman and congresswomen, and all the thousands of people on their staffs for creating the program, or the millions of dollars in costs to society caused by the all the other urgent problems they *didn't* solve during those thousands of man-hours they spent over those four years creating the program, or the millions of dollars in wages for the thousands of people will have to be hired to administer the program, or the millions of dollars and logistics it will take for them to get the job done, or the millions of dollars in fraud, waste and abuse committed by people who use the program to get a new backboard when theirs wasn't really broken in the first place, (because after all, it's *free* isn't it? It doesn't really cost anything to anyone, so why shouldn't we get our slice of the pie? Isn't that why we elected that congressman in the first place, to get us our stuff?), or the millions of dollars in wages to the thousands of people who will need to be hired to try to root out all that fraud waste and abuse, or the millions of dollars in wages for the thousands of people who will have to be hired to enforce those 159 pages of regulations, or the millions of dollars it will take to prosecute the dangerous criminal masterminds who will conspire to violate those regulations.

Yeah, if you don't count all of *that*, *it's free!*

Okay, if you want to get technical about it, it's not exactly free. It will be paid for by raising taxes, on everyone in the country, for all eternity, but it's only a *little bit* of tax for each of us. You probably won't even notice it, and even if you do, you didn't really *need* that date night dinner with your spouse, did you?

Well, Okay if you really want to get nasty and split hairs, it won't actually be paid for by the new taxes because *that* money actually got diverted to pay a subsidy to a soybean farmer who had a contract with a biofuels company in Idaho. It was in the bill, on page 732. Didn't you read it? Well, that's okay, neither did your senator or your congressman, or anyone else who voted on it. Yes, the company did get the subsidy for that farmer because it made a generous contribution to that congressman's reelection campaign, and yes, the company did go bankrupt a month later, but hey, they were trying to save the planet, man! You don't *want* them to save the earth? Why do you hate the earth?

So the federal basketball goal program will actually be paid for by our country going just a little farther into debt, but it's only a *little bit* more for each of us, and after all, *it's for the children!* You don't want the children to have a new basketball goal? Why do you hate the children? You're just so full of hate!

So that's the second plan. Oh, there's one more thing I should mention. On page 1,162 of the bill, there's a provision that outlaws any subsequent Hometown Plans. So from now on, the only way anyone will be able to get a new basketball goal is through the Proving We Love Our Children Through Affordable Basketball Goals Act, because after all, something *this* important really should be in the hands of our country's best and brightest minds.

In my first draft of this chapter, I had several questions for you comparing the two plans, but at this point, I really do think the answers are so obvious it would be silly to ask them except for one: Which of these plans will leave everyone involved with a greater sense of community and connection to each other?

If I haven't made my point clear, here it is: The lower the level of government at which something can be accomplished, the better things turn out for everyone. If you can keep the government out of it altogether, even better, because *government is the most expensive, least efficient, least effective, and most intrusive, not to mention the* **slowest** *way to get anything done.* Take a couple of minutes to really consider the implications of that statement. When I say "most expensive", that implies there is a *less expensive* way. When I say "least effective", that means there is a *more effective* way. When I say "least efficient and most intrusive" that means there's a *more efficient* and *less intrusive* way to do it. Now be honest with me and honest with yourself: When I tell you there's a less expensive, more efficient, more effective, less intrusive and faster way to do something; when I tell you there are five different kinds of *a better way to do it*, does it really, truly sound to you like *I don't want it done?* I didn't think so. Good, maybe we can at least begin to put that particular lie to rest.

If you think this concept would apply only to basketball and nothing else, you are seriously deluding yourself. The concept applies to any decision-making process or action that government is capable of taking. When you get to the level where you're dealing with serious laws, and breaking them involves big fines being imposed and prison sentences handed down, the impact on people's lives is even greater. Can you imagine what this Country would be like if we went with the Hometown Plan whenever it was possible?

Before we consider doing anything at the Federal level, we should ask ourselves, can it be accomplished at the state level? If it can, then we should seriously ask, can it be accomplished at the County level, because State Government is the most expensive, least efficient, least effective, most intrusive and slowest way to get anything done *at the state level.* If we can accomplish it at the county level, we should seriously consider whether or not it can be accomplished at the municipal level, because there is no logical reason why a city ordinance prohibiting an activity, with a penalty sufficient to discourage people from doing it, would *not* be every bit as effective *in that city* as a federal law prohibiting the same activity.

If an ordinance is adopted in some cities and not in others, it's because the people in those other cities simply don't feel it's a pressing enough issue for them, and they don't want to live under a new law designed to solve *someone else's* problem. If it *is* adopted, the city councilman who drafted it will have to deal with the consequences, good and bad, of the new ordinance right alongside their fellow citizens and be held immediately accountable to them. That is of course, unless they decide to behave like Congress, and tell their constituents, "Hey, *you* have to live under the laws we pass, *we* don't." But then again when their constituents live three miles from their front door and not 3000, what are the chances of them getting away with that?

Are there some issues that *must* be dealt with on a nationwide basis? Of course there are. I'd be willing to bet there are as many as.... *eighteen* of them, but how do we go about determining exactly what those eighteen things are? Well, that's already been done for us by a group extremely capable people; people who were on average one hell of a lot more educated and knowledgeable about the way the world has actually worked throughout history than today's average congressman or senator; people who (gasp) actually *read* things they had written *before* they voted on them! You can find a really nifty list of those eighteen things in a place called Article 1, Section 8, of a crazy little document *I* like to call, the United States Constitution.

If, after reading all of this, you are still utterly convinced that *everything* absolutely must be dealt with in Washington, because there is simply no one, anywhere, in any of the fifty states who is smart enough and capable enough to get the job done, I'll ask you this one last question: *Where on Earth do you think the people in Washington came from?*

The Last Chapter

After writing an entire book on politics, and that's actually what *all* the chapters, including the ones on religion and sex ultimately deal with, I have a confession to make: Every once in a while, I get thoroughly sick of talking about it. It *is* important to be involved in the decisions that effect our lives, and knowledgeable about the ideas behind those decisions, but too often politics unnecessarily comes between us. It raises our blood pressure, makes our hands shake and the veins pop out on our foreheads. If we let it go too far, it ruins friendships, and damages relationships with family members, and it should never be allowed to do that.

So for the last chapter of this book, I'd like to just step away from it, forget all about it, and just wrap things up by having a little bit of totally inconsequential fun. So for the last few pages, let's imagine we're getting outside in the fresh air, strolling down a country lane, forgetting all our troubles for a little while, and talking   about....

Bigfoot!

I'm a huge Bigfoot aficionado. I even have a "Gone Squatchin" T-shirt. Finding Bigfoot on Animal Planet used to be one of my favorite TV shows. I watched it from its debut and I never missed an episode....that is, until I realized something; the people on that show are *never* going to find Bigfoot. The producers of Finding Bigfoot are not in the business of finding cryptids, they're in the business of producing a television show, on schedule, week after week, and the investigators on the show are in the business of earning a paycheck from it. They really should rename the show "Not Finding Bigfoot."

So now I'm going to insist that Bigfoot exists, right? Wrong, because Bigfoot just doesn't exist. Common sense and logic dictate that Bigfoot is just a figment of overactive imaginations. The most glaringly obvious fact excluding the possibility of its existence is, this is the 21st-century, for crying out loud. The earth has been thoroughly explored. We have mapped every square inch of it from space, and any remaining large animals have long since been discovered by science. Bigfoot isn't among them, so Bigfoot doesn't exist.

Of course, neither did the Giant Panda until 1869, when suddenly it did exist.

And neither did the Okapi, a 6-foot tall, 550-pound relative of the giraffe until 1901, when suddenly, it did exist.

And neither did the Mountain Gorilla until 1902, when suddenly it did.

And neither did the 7-foot-long, 650-pound Giant Forest Hog of Africa until 1904, when suddenly it did.

Neither did the Komodo Dragon, the World's largest lizard until 1910, when suddenly it did.

Neither did the Koupry, a 7-foot long, 2000-pound bovine native to Southeast Asia until 1937, when suddenly it did.

Neither did the Coelacanth, a big, smelly, 7-foot long fish until 1938, when suddenly it did.

Neither did the 16 foot long, 2600-pound Megamouth Shark until 1975, when suddenly it did.

Neither did the Chacoan Peccary, the largest species of peccary in the world until 1975, when suddenly it did.

Neither did the 100-pound Giant Muntjac Deer of Vietnam until 1994, when suddenly it did.

Neither did the Rewoche Horse of Tibet until 1995, when suddenly it did.

Neither did the Bili Ape, a gorilla sized chimpanzee of the Congo until 2003, when suddenly it did.

And neither did Burchell's Zebra until 2004, when suddenly it *did* exist.

My, oh my. So many species of large animals just suddenly springing into existence out of thin air. Rather peculiar but completely understandable, because we all know that nothing *really exists* until it's been "recognized by science."

But putting all that aside, there are still a plethora of a well reasoned, insightful arguments against the existence of Bigfoot, all put forth by very smart people, many of whom have never set foot off a university campus and into the wilderness, where the stuff they're expounding upon....you know....*actually happens.* Let's review a few of them just to reassure ourselves of our obvious intellectual superiority:

"If a creature that big were running around the North American countryside, someone would've *seen* it by now."

You'd think so, huh? The last time I counted (and I did count) the Bigfoot Field Researchers Organization alone had over 4,700 sighting reports in their database for North America excluding Mexico. Other organizations and individuals have their own databases with thousands more. Then, there are the legends of countless Aboriginal American tribes, passed down through generations for thousands of years. (But you can discount those, can't you? After all, they're just legends, told by *Indians,* and that's not a least bit racist thing to say, is it?) I think it's safe to say that someone *has* seen Bigfoot. Plus, you have to consider this: If *you* saw Bigfoot, would *you* tell anyone? For a lot of people, the answer is no, because unlike me, they're actually concerned about their reputations, so it's logical to assume there are a certain number of sightings that go unreported.

"Yeah, well all of those sightings were a guy in a monkey suit."

Yeah, all those multiple thousands of them. The majority of the sightings are of an animal 7 to 10 feet tall. Do you know how many 7-foot tall people there are in the United States? Well, according to Sports Illustrated Magazine, citing data from the Centers for Disease Control, there are about 70 of them, and 30 of them are playing in the NBA, so that leaves 40 candidates. 40 people responsible for thousands of Bigfoot sightings over hundreds of years.... sure, that's doable. Do you know how many 8-foot tall people there are in the world? Three. One lives in Turkey, one lives in Morocco, and one in Iraq. Do you know how many Nine-foot tall people there are in the world? Zero.

Those forty or so guys who are responsible for all this Bigfoot nonsense should be easy to track down with a little financial detective work, because they're probably all independently wealthy. They'd have to be to make a full-time occupation of trekking into the most remote forests and mountains in the country and then just sort of hanging out there in their state-of-the-art monkey suits for indefinite periods of time, on the off chance that someone might come wandering by. You know what we're *not* seeing though? The helicopters, which must be kept busy day and night flying them around the wilderness and dropping them off for all of these chance encounters, hundreds of miles and sometimes only hours apart.

And while we're at it, *how about those monkey suits?* If there are thousands of sightings, it stands to reason there must be *at least* dozens of suits. Well...where are they? Of all the people who have claimed to actually be the guy in the suit, and there have been dozens of them, not a single one has ever been able to pull the suit out of their closet and show it to the media. I guess they must be stashed away along with all the carved wooden feet used to fake the footprints.

Ah yes, there are all of those footprints; *thousands* of them.

"Easy. Like you just said, those are all made by guys who carved wooden feet and strapped them to their boots."

Yeah, except that the footprints being found show signs of bending and flexing around rocks and sticks that are stepped on, and while going up and down hills. Many of them also have dermal ridges; the pedal equivalent of fingerprints and just as unique. And, the guys who carved them must've studied various known and visually diagnosable orthopedic disorders and then extrapolated how those would manifest themselves in the feet of animals that don't exist, because those have been found too. When you walk down a beach and look back at your footprints, you will see a little ridges of sand pushed up right behind the balls of your feet. Those little ridges are also found wherever Bigfoot footprints are found in any terrain that's conducive to them. Try re-creating *that* with rigid wooden feet. Another interesting characteristic of these footprints is something called the Mid-Tarsal Break. It amounts to a pseudo-joint in the middle of the foot, allowing it to flex as the animal steps off of it. Humans obviously don't have a Mid-Tarsal break, *but gorillas do.* Interesting.

"Well, footprints aren't really evidence of the presence of a species."

Don't you mean *Bigfoot* footprints aren't really evidence of the presence of *Bigfoot?* I ask this because, if you found hundreds of elk tracks in a meadow, would you insist that there is no evidence of elk in the area? Wildlife biologists actually base some yearly animal census counts on tracks alone.

Here's another really interesting thing. Take any characteristic of a living animal; physical or otherwise: Height, weight, hair density, age, intelligence level, foot length; any characteristic you can name. If you plot all of the data for a population of that animal on a graph, you'll get a Bell Curve. If it's for human height, you get very few really short people on one end, lots of average sized people in the middle, and a few very tall ones on the other end. The Bell Curve is so ubiquitous that it's also known as the Normal Distribution.

Now, take any alleged reported characteristic of Bigfoot; height, hair color, foot size, foot length to width ratio, stride length, any characteristic for which physical evidence *has* been found, and take all of the data (uh, excuse me....*alleged data*, gathered by certifiable nut cases) and plot it on the same kind of graph. Do you know what you'll get? That's right, a *Bell Curve*. Again.... interesting.

And while we're on the subject of physical evidence, how about the hair? Numerous specimens have been found and sent to reputable laboratories for DNA analysis. Every time, the result has been that the specimen comes from an "unknown primate."

"Well those hairs came from a gorilla, or something like that."

..........(Temporarily speechless).........Hoooo-kaayyyy! So now we have **gorillas** in North America, which no one *ever* sees, but we *don't* have Bigfoots, which thousands of people *have* seen. These arguments are just making more sense by the minute.

But you know.... I'm kind of thinking a gorilla would be a *known* primate. Yeah, the more I think about it, I'm pretty sure gorillas are in the database. This is why you never hear conservationists say "There are less than 800 unknown primates left in the mountains of central Africa. I mean, they *were* gorillas, but we sent some of their hair to a lab and the results came back "unknown primate", so now we're not so sure. But you know what, you should just believe everything we say anyway; because we're *scientists* and that means we're just a whole heck of a lot smarter than you are. After all, weren't we the ones who told you that the Black Footed Ferret and the Coelacanth were both extinct? I mean hey, come on, what better credentials could you want than *that?*"

"If Bigfoots exist, why don't they appear in the fossil record?"

Neither chimpanzees nor gorillas were ever found in the fossil record until 2016….and yet, they *existed for millions of years before that.* Next!

"Okay, but you have to consider the source. I mean, Bigfoots are only seen by hillbillies, yahoos, rednecks and tin-foil hatters, right?"

Right. Hillbillies, yahoos, rednecks and tin-foil hatters….and professional hunters, outfitters and trackers, law-enforcement officials, military officers, wildlife biologists, archaeologists, documentary filmmakers and wilderness survival experts; people with fairly respectable credentials who are in many cases also trained to make accurate observations.

"Well, how come none of them ever caught it on video?"

Actually, dozens of people have captured video of what they saw, but even if they didn't, let's do a little thought experiment. I'm going to give you a video camera. We'll either put it in your pack or hang it around your neck, but either way it will probably be turned off most of the time because holding it up to your eye all the time makes your face and arm hurt, and keeping it on standby burns the battery up real quick. Then, we'll put you in an environment that I know intimately and you don't, where there are dozens of places for me to hide, the nearest one of them never more than a few seconds away. Now I'm going to hide somewhere in that environment (you won't know where.) I'll let you discover me at some point (you won't know when), and the second *I* see *you,* I'm going to hightail it out of there as fast as I can. (Oh, did I mention that I'll basically be camouflaged in natural earth tones? Well, I will.) Now, do you really think you can get that camera out, turn it on, wait for it to boot up and then catch good video footage of me if I really don't want you to? Of course you can, because you're not a hillbilly, a yahoo, a redneck *or* a tin-foil hatter, are ya?

"Well then, how come there's so much good footage of other animals? You know, grizzly bears and bighorn sheep and what-not?"

I'll let you in on a little secret. The overwhelming majority of footage you see in wildlife documentaries is of captive animals on wildlife preserves. Many of the animals are domesticated. Most of the grizzly bear footage we adults saw as kids was actually the same bear, and his name was Bart. I'll tell you what; I'll let you keep the video camera and give you a *month*, and then let's see if *you* can bring me back some really good, clear footage of a mountain lion or a wolverine, or better yet, a bobcat. Plenty of people go into the wilderness hundreds of times over the course of their lives hoping to catch just a glimpse of a mountain lion and *never do*. One professional wildlife film crew spent weeks in the wild intending to capture video of a wild wolverine. After three weeks with a professional guide, a few frames showing a small brown dot in the middle of a field of snow was all they got.

"Yeah, well the people who thought they saw Bigfoot were just seeing some other animal and misidentifying it".

Here's what I find interesting: let's just take a subset of these people, excluding the yahoos. Now as I said, many of these people are trained to make accurate observations and for others, the professional hunters, outfitters and trackers in particular, their livelihoods depend on making accurate observations. One of the most crucial things hunters do before even thinking about pulling the trigger is positively identifying their targets as well as what's beyond them. They tend to get slapped with very big fines and maybe even jail time if they don't. Now, if one of *those* people told you they saw a moose, would you automatically assume that they really saw an elk and just misidentified it as it moose? If one of them told you they saw a mule deer, would you automatically assume they actually saw a black bear and just misidentified it as a mule deer? If one of them told you they saw a musk ox, would you automatically assume they actually saw a wood bison and just misidentified it as a musk ox? Ha! Trick question! Wood bison and musk oxen don't have overlapping ranges!

So, am I to understand that you believe these people *can* tell a moose, from an elk, from a mule deer, from a black bear, from a musk oxen, from a wood bison, from any other of the dozens of species of large animals out there, but collectively, they *can't distinguish any* of them from a nine foot tall, humanoid shaped creature with long arms, hands, square shoulders, no neck and a vaguely human looking face? Okay, I guess you're better at making those calls than they are, sitting in your urban living room or your university cubicle. Why did I ever doubt you?

"Well I've heard that big hairy things are something we're psychologically programed to see. Something about genetic memory, or something like that."

Okay, fine, we are genetically predisposed to see them. Then why do we *never* see them in dark alleyways or in city parks, or in subway tunnels, or in the darkened hallways of apartment buildings for that matter? If seeing big hairy creatures is something people are just naturally programed to do, then where there are *more* people, there will be *more* sightings, and where there are the *most* people, there will be the *most* sightings. Therefore, if this theory were correct, the biggest hotbeds of Bigfoot activity would be New York, Chicago and Los Angeles....

....but *not* Honolulu. Bigfoots have been sighted in every state in the United States, *except Hawaii.* No sightings there...zero, zilch, zip, nada, ever. You remember Hawaii dont'cha? The state that's isolated out there in the middle of the ocean? The only state you *can't walk to?* I can't explain to you right now the exact scientific process by which being located across an un-swimmable expanse of water deletes a specific genetic memory from an entire population, but I'll get right on it and get back to you.

"Well people who see Bigfoot are just imagining it. There's nothing to be embarrassed about. It's just something people do once in a while. No big deal."

You're right. Imagination can be a very powerful thing. Just think; J.K. Rowling *imagined* Hogwarts. J.R.R. Tolkien *imagined* Middle Earth. If they could imagine entire worlds, then it's not so hard to believe that a person could imagine seeing a Bigfoot. There's just one little problem: *Imagination* is a *willful* process. J.K. Rowling imagined the world of Harry Potter because she made a conscious and deliberate decision to do so. J.R.R. Tolkien spent thousands of hours of disciplined effort to imagine every detail of Middle Earth. Imagination is not something that randomly hijacks a person's cognitive processes and *makes* them see things that aren't there. That's not called imagination, that's called *hallucination,* and if you're proposing that hallucinating is just something humans do once in a while, and it's no big deal, nothing to be embarrassed about, I would urge you to consider the implications to civilization from people such as air traffic controllers, brain surgeons, police officers and battlefield commanders.

"Yeah, well Bigfoot's are only seen by hillbillies, yahoos, rednecks and tin-foil hatters."

That's right; *if you can't disprove the message, discredit the messenger.* Hey, it works in politics, so why not here? But we're not doing politics right now, we're just having some fun, *and* disproving the existence of Bigfoot.

Okay, I'm going to make one last attempt to bring some sanity to this discussion. I'm going to bring out the big guns. Say hello to my friend and yours, Occam's Razor. For those of you who are not familiar, Occam's Razor is a "principle of parsimony, economy, or succinctness" named after William Ockham, an influential medieval philosopher and nominalist, though he certainly wasn't the first to come up with the idea. It was the scientific precept used by the mainstream science community, along with the government to discredit Jodie Foster's character in the excellent science-fiction movie Contact, after her first contact experience in that film.

Occam's Razor states that among competing hypotheses, the one that makes the fewest assumptions should be selected. In a more popular wording, it says: "All other things being equal, the simplest explanation tends to be the correct one." It's a valuable scientific precept, and has served men of science well for hundreds of years in cutting through all the gobbledygook that can stand in the way of scientific progress. So, let's apply it to this discussion about Bigfoot.

Explanation Number One: There is a multi-generational secret society of acromegalic multi-millionaires, who carefully choose their members for specific physical attributes so as to conform to a Normal Distribution, are equipped with the latest in state-of-the-art make up and Hollywood costume technology including unique dermal ridge patterns on the feet of their costumes, which are also made with just the right variety of physical variations so as to also conform to a Normal Distribution, and are kept under lock and key so the public never sees them, ever, and who also collectively possess such a unique talent for remote assessment of human character that they are able to selectively reveal themselves only to hillbillies, yahoos, rednecks, tin-foil hatters and other trained and experienced individuals who, despite spending extensive hours in the wilderness observing nature, are unable to distinguish between species of large animals, and who, just for good measure, volunteer to have the bones in their feet broken and reset using revolutionary new medical technologies in order to simulate the footprints of non-human primates that don't exist.

Explanation Number Two: There is a rare, elusive, largely nocturnal, yet to be officially discovered, bipedal primate living in North America.

Hmmmmmmm....This *is* a tricky one, but after much consideration, I have to conclude that ***Explanation Number One is much simpler!***

So there you have it. Bigfoot is a myth. I'm glad we were able to finally put this to rest. Good work!

Author's Note

The era of the gatekeepers is over. With platforms like Kindle, CD Baby, YouTube and CreateSpace, independent authors and musicians like myself no longer have to supplicate themselves before huge, powerful publishing houses and record companies that care nothing about them, and everything about the bottom line, and that's a *good* thing. Talk about "Power to the People?" Well, *this is it!*

But there's also a downside to the democratization of digital media, and that is that independent authors and musicians like myself don't have access to the huge advertising budgets the gatekeepers still have, and we probably never will. That's why we have to ask for just a little bit of your help. If you enjoyed this book and think the ideas in it are worthy of being passed on, tell a couple of your friends about it. On second thought, what the heck, tell *all* of them about it! If you *really* enjoyed it, please consider writing a review on Amazon.

On the other hand, if you absolutely *hated* this book and think I'm an idiot, *tell all of your friends about it, so that they can see what an idiot I am as well!* And, if you feel absolutely compelled to publicly denounce me, I ask only one thing: *Denounce me in as loud and persistent a voice as you can!*

I thoroughly enjoyed writing this book and I hope you enjoyed reading it, but just as much, I enjoyed the process of looking at the world with the questioning and critical eye that inspired me to write it, and I hope starting here and now, it inspires just a little of that in you.